NUMERIC RELATIONSHIPS
 a beginner's guide

JOHN C. BURFORD

Hodder & Stoughton
A MEMBER OF THE HODDER HEADLINE GROUP

Orders: please contact Bookpoint Ltd, 78 Milton Park, Abingdon, Oxon OX14 4TD.
Telephone: (44) 01235 827720, Fax: (44) 01235 400454. Lines are open from
9.00–6.00, Monday to Saturday, with a 24 hour message answering service.
Email address: orders@bookpoint.co.uk

British Library Cataloguing in Publication Data
A catalogue record for this title is available from The British Library

ISBN 0 340 77487 8

First published 1998
This edition published 2000
Impression number 10 9 8 7 6 5 4 3 2 1
Year   2005 2004 2003 2002 2001 2000 1999

Typeset by Transet Limited, Coventry, England.
Printed in Great Britain for Hodder & Stoughton Educational, a division of Hodder
Headline plc, 338 Euston Road, London NW1 3BH by Cox and Wyman Limited,
Reading, Berks.

CONTENTS

FOREWORD

A good name is better than precious ointment.

The Book of Ecclesiastes VII, 1

Nomen est omen, said the ancient Romans and, as a numerologist, I must agree that our name is, indeed, our destiny. Who can doubt, for instance, that if the famous film actor Cary Grant has not changed his name from Archibald Leach, he almost certainly would not have achieved his great success? He established his career playing mainly romantic leads. Do you think any of his leading ladies could have kept a straight face as they kissed Archibald Leach? Probably not.

Our names are **not** an arbitrary means of identification. They were not chosen at random by our parents, who may have used a name book, taken our name from a personality of the time or from family tradition. However, at some deeper level, they knew exactly what to call us. How can I make such a bold statement? Because numerology holds the key to unlocking the wisdom in our names – our names contain hidden (esoteric) information about our character, our often hidden yearnings and our destiny. It also holds the key to understanding our relationships.

We humans are complex beings – often a mass of contradictions. Numerology is a means of finding order within the chaos. Even so it cannot explain every facet of us or our relationships. It is important to keep in mind that, within any relationship, there are indefinable links that we may never be able to understand. How often have we said of a relationship: I wonder what she sees in him (and *vice versa*)?

Numerology is a simple method of highlighting the important energies and potentials within each of us and within our relationships.

If you are sceptical about the validity of the subject, then all I ask is for you to apply the methods I describe and see for yourself whether or not they work for you. This is the test of what I am about to reveal. Numerology is an ancient science. It posits that numbers are symbols for universal energies or vibrations. We carry our own personal energies in the numbers of our names and our birthdates. As the ideas of modern physics and ancient traditions come closer together, we see that the whole universe is an ever changing structure of energies of various kinds. Try to keep that idea in mind as you work through this book – try to see numbers as representing energies and issues when you construct your own chart and that of others. You may never see numbers in the same light again.

There have been several pioneer numerologists who have made valuable contributions to our understanding of ourselves. In this book I bring together, perhaps for the first time, several methods that can help us in our understanding of our relationships. For most of us, it is our intimate relationships that provide our greatest joys and greatest disappointments, whether these relationships are with our parents, children, or partners. It is my sincere wish that this book will help you gain a better understanding of yourself and your relationships and help you achieve a greater sense of purpose, thereby putting you in harmony with the universe.

Only a very moderate level of mathematical skill is required to work with these methods and, in fact, every method described can be worked out on the back of an envelope – no computers are necessary! If you wish to gain proficiency, just remember what the old New Yorker advised when asked by a young man, carrying a violin case, how to get to Carnegie Hall: 'Practice, my son, Practice'.

John C. Burford
Autumn 1997

INTRODUCTION

We can have a relationship with many people – our parents, our brothers/sisters, our cousins/nieces, our spouse, our partner, our children, our work colleagues, business contacts, etc. Many readers will be interested in learning of their love partners and the material in this book will be applicable to such relationships. For other relationships, most of the material will still apply and, in order to avoid awkward presentation, I am using the word 'partner' to describe the other party in a relationship.

Numbers dominate our Lives

Few of us recognise the extent to which names and numbers dominate our lives. We have telephone numbers, bank account numbers, credit card numbers, house numbers, birthdays, TV and radio station numbers, date and time of the day numbers. Our names are numbered according to the position of each letter in the alphabet. Most of us take the alphabet for granted, having learned it by rote at school. But it is clear that the sequence of the 26 letters – A,B,C, ... X,Y,Z is not a random arrangement dreamed up by some scribe long ago. In fact, our alphabet is a carefully compiled list (created over many centuries) of a progression of symbolic elements, each of which is reflected in the numerical value of each letter. The ancient Romans used letters to represent numbers (I=1; V=5; X=10; L=50; C=100; D=500; M=1,000), so they understood that, in some ways, numbers and letters were connected.

Most of us seek answers to the basic questions of existence – Why am I here? – What am I here to do? – How can I accomplish my tasks? Character analysis through numerology can offer specific answers. Our lives are a progression of learning experiences in order to gain wisdom. Sometimes these experiences are very painful and we must struggle to get ahead while at other times, we find the going easy. **Numerology can indicate, from our name and birthdate, the blueprint for our life**.

Relationships are mirrors to see ourselves

Along life's journey we meet many people and have close relationships with some. Our parents, our brothers or sisters, our school friends, our love partners and then our children all provide us with many vivid opportunities to allow another person into our most intimate space. Perhaps 'allow' isn't always the right word – some of us have weak boundaries where a strong parent, for instance, can seem to dominate us. Then we have some often difficult lessons to learn about the limits we place on our responsibilities.

If we have been hurt in our early years we may withdraw into our shell, others find it difficult to get close to us, our relationships are often superficial or of short duration and may be fraught with conflicts. Then we feel no one loves us, but we fail to acknowledge our part in this – we have often brought it upon ourselves. Unfortunately, some people live most of their lives in this closed-up state, afraid to come out of their shell. In their determination never to get hurt again, they shut off all possibilities of an intimate relationship. They are then living only part of their life, since to live life fully means being prepared to risk being hurt and disappointed. Such a person needs to be shown, gently, how to open up to life and numerology can offer help with this.

Our relationships with others can be seen as a reflection of ourselves and we often do not like what we see. If we are irritated by something our partner (or parent, friend, sibling) does or says we may criticise

them and, thereby, provoke an argument, However, since the relationship is a mirror, what we see is usually that part of ourselves that we have hidden and dislike. We are really having an argument with ourselves. Does this make sense?

If we wish to improve our relationships, then we must start by understanding what makes us and our partner tick – and we can do this by employing the numerology concepts in this book. Then, to make a real difference, we must be willing to use the energies indicated by our name and birthdate in a positive way. Knowing the requirements and possibilities indicated by your Personal Years (see Chapter 4) and the Personal Year of your partner, is important information to help you 'swim with the tide'. For instance, in an inner, reflective, Personal Seven Year it is normally unwise to become involved in lots of social activities. A partner may be in a socially active Personal Three Year and, if we do not understand the real needs of ourselves and our partners, we may have difficulties reconciling our different needs.

REINCARNATION

Many of us have asked the question: What happens to us after we die? Let us ask another question at the same time: What happens to us before we are born? The idea of reincarnation (literally: *coming back in a body*) gives us answers to both questions.

If we agree that we are here on earth to learn and grow towards a state of perfection (wisdom) we must be incarnated many times and, if we agree that the universe (including ourselves) is made up of **energy** of various kinds and frequencies, we know from physics that energy cannot be created or destroyed. Therefore, as individuals, we cannot be created or destroyed. Our bodies, of course, pass through the natural cycle of conception, birth, growth, maturity and then death. But our essence (or spirit) is indestructible – and it is our spirit that directs our experiences on earth.

Karma is the universal law of cause and effect. If we, in previous lives, have neglected or mistreated others we may, in this life, be

3

asked to 'balance the books'. This may involve us with lots of sacrifices. **Numerology gives specific insights into our karma in this lifetime from our name** (more of this in Chapter 3). Our karma can deeply affect our relationships.

WHAT WE ARE ARE BORN WITH

Science tells us that we inherit half of our genes from our mother and half from our father. Our genes direct the way in which we grow and develop. However much we try, we cannot shake off the strong biological and soul links with our parents. The expression 'blood is thicker than water' reflects this fact. We are not clones of either – we have our own Life Path and Destiny – and our own free will. The numbers contained in our names represent the potentials and energies we are born with. The rest we make up.

THE NUMBERS AND CHALLENGES HIDDEN IN A NAME

For the numerical values of the letters, see Table 1.

In many societies, children take their father's family name. Let us say that Peter and Ann Smith have a child which they call Emma. She is known as Emma Smith. Emma has the energies of both names; **Emma** (5 + 4 + 4 = 14 = **5**) and **Smith** (1 + 4 + 9 + 2 + 8 = 24 = **6**). The name Smith, therefore, has the energy of the Six and runs throughout the family. Because the Six is the number of love, of home, family duty, responsibility and caring, all members of the Smith family will be to some extent people with a strong sense of family ties.

Emma also carries the Five energy in her first name. This is the number of movement, of experiencing life fully. So Emma will have some hard choices to make – whether to follow her yearning to travel and to move home (from her restless Five energy of 'Emma') – or to stay at home curled up reading a book by the fire (from her stay-at-home Six energy of 'Smith').

From her name alone, we can tell that Emma may have difficulties, especially in her teenage years, when separation from parents naturally becomes a dominant force. It would take understanding parents to help Emma through these decisions.

EXERCISE: WHAT IS THE ENERGY OF YOUR FAMILY NAME?

From Table 1 (see p. 26) work out the energy of your family name:

YOUR FAMILY NAME:

EXAMPLE:
Your family name is SPENCER

S 1
P 7
E 5
N 5
C 3
E 5
R 9

TOTAL ....

TOTAL 35

Now reduce to a 'Root' Number:
....

Now reduce to a 'Root' Number:
3 plus 5 equals **8**

Now look at the energies of Your Number in Chapter 1.

Now look at the energies of the Number Eight in Chapter 1.

Answer:

Answer: The Eight energy is one of authority and power (over people). Therefore, someone with the Spencer name has a tendency to rise to the top and exert authority over others.

1

BASIC CONCEPTS
IN NUMEROLOGY

BRIEF HISTORY OF NUMEROLOGY

Pythagorus, who was born in Greece in about 600 BC, is widely seen as the 'Father of Numerology'. His is an interesting story. He was given his name by the Oracle at Delphi and, when a young child, entered one of the Temples for a very wide-ranging education. He studied meditation, the sciences, and was a great athlete, winning prizes at the Olympic Games. It is said that he formulated the idea that the earth was a sphere which revolved around the sun. He is mostly remembered today for his famous Theorem concerning the relationship between the sides of a right-angled triangle.

He was a charismatic character and, after a series of initiations, was given the name of Yarancharya (he considered the letter Y very mystical). He organised a school in Crotona and taught there for nearly forty years. He taught in secret forbidding students to write notes of any kind. Only after his death were some of his teachings revealed to the outside world.

He taught that nature expresses geometry with mathematical precision, that the relationship of experience to numbers is Divine Law and that is the basis of character analysis through numerology. He also taught that the letters of the alphabet were associated with numbers.

Modern numerology uses these ideas of Pythagorus and our alphabet is an exact and accurate mathematical sequence of numbers. There is an exact correspondence of the letters of the alphabet and the numbers – a surprising idea to those that have not given either our alphabet or our numbers much thought.

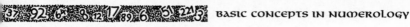

We also use the 10–base number system which probably originated with the Hindu-Arabic mathematicians of the eighth to tenth centuries BC. Ancient Egyptians also used the 10–base system. Our modern method of number notation was developed by the famous mathematician Fibonacci around AD 1200.

The esoteric meaning of numbers

Study of numerology starts with the first nine numbers – the **Root Numbers** (see *Numerology for Beginners* by Kristyna Arcarti in this series). These comprise all the numbers of the world, for all following numbers are **Compound Numbers** and are variants of the original nine root numbers. The zero is not considered a true number, but when it appears, it intensifies the associated number. In this book we shall explain how numbers apply to people and especially to their relationships.

It is immediately clear that not all numbers are benevolent and it is important to remember this fact. Also, when we discuss the characteristics of numbers, we are talking about archetypes. Few, if any, humans are archetypical, but an interesting mixture of several types. So, if you discover that your Life Purpose is 4, the temptation is to say: 'I am a Four'. However, no one is a number and your full chart will probably show other important influences as well.

Whether you view a number as being 'good' or 'bad' depends on your attitude and free will. If you look at life in a negative way, then you will see some numbers as being 'bad' and indicative of your fate. If you look at life in a positive way, then you may see some numbers as being unfortunate, but with the *potential* to be redeemable, given some effort and some change in thought patterns. There is no 'right' or 'wrong' way to see numbers and their meanings. What we are attempting to see with numerology is the way things really are. When we see ourselves a little more clearly, we can see our partners more clearly and our relationships deepen.

One further point about the numbers – when we talk of a number being 'masculine' or 'feminine', we mean that the number has either masculine or feminine *characteristics* as opposed to being 'male' or 'female'. Therefore, a woman can have strong masculine energies, as revealed by the numbers of her chart.

Let us now examine the meaning of the nine Root Numbers, particularly as they apply to love relationships.

Suggestion: You may wish to return to this part after you have learned how to discover your Life Path Number and Life Purpose Number in Chapter 2.

THE NUMBER 1

The Number One deals with **creation** ('In the beginning…'). It is the number of **action**. It is an intelligent force with courage, daring and will. It seeks to invent, explore and create something where nothing has previously existed. It sets the pattern for others to follow – it is a **leader**. It often goes where angels fear to tread.

It is the initiator of intelligent action. It doesn't wait for others to be persuaded; it just goes ahead, often unconcerned whether anyone is following or not. Without the One, we would have no progress. It is the archetypal **masculine** number, ruled by the **Sun**.

THE NUMBER 1 IN RELATIONSHIPS

The Number One is interesting to be with and is a good companion. They are usually pleasant with a good sense of humour. They are often the life and soul of the party and can be relied upon to liven up proceedings when things get a little dull. Very often, they hold strong opinions on just about everything under the sun. However, their strong character is expressed with dignity and sensitivity and they have a good sense of taste. To others, they can seem strangely different, as if they have a secret mission in life.

They are very attracted to the opposite sex, beauty, a strong personality and someone with high self-confidence. They reject dullness and the ordinary. They dislike a partner who is too demanding as they, themselves, want to do the demanding (often without realising it).

Within partnerships, the Number One requires a great deal of understanding and must be drawn towards the positive subtly by their partner. If their partner criticises too much, the One often withdraws into their shell and stubbornly refuses to co-operate, sometimes displaying uncharacteristic cynicism and temper. If there is too much criticism, the One loses self-confidence and appears shy, weak and afraid to express how they truly feel. Partners should avoid criticism of the One and approach mutual difficulties together so that the One may use their natural creative talents to overcome their difficulties. When the One is being 'macho' and aggressive, it is a sure sign that they are out of touch with self-confidence and feel alone.

The Number One requires a loving partner, who is strong and non-demanding. They have lots to give and respond well to loving support. Without adequate support, care and affection in the home, Ones will very often not achieve great happiness and success. Quite possibly, the expression: 'Behind every great man there is a woman' was coined for male Ones.

Ones are driven by a strict adherence to high standards of behaviour and personal appearance, hygiene and fitness. They can, in fact, be almost fanatical in these areas. Consequently, they can be very difficult to live with and, if their partner does not share these same standards, the One will often retreat from the unattractive, sometimes taking to addictive behaviour. In fact, Ones make the best addicts (smoking, drugs, food, sex, etc.) if they lose their self-control. In this case, the One needs to direct their prodigious creative urges into more positive outlets.

The One would like to win the argument, but would rather be the Boss.

Key Energies:
- independence
- originality
- leadership
- stubbornness
- secure/insecure

THE NUMBER 2

The Number Two is a 'Yes' person. Nothing is too much trouble for a Number Two and, often, they will give without being asked. They speak when they are spoken to and would rather die than utter a firm opinion, especially when it would 'rock the boat'. It is the number of **passivity**. It seeks to please others, to 'go with the flow', to pour oil onto troubled waters (often created by a One) – it is a **follower**. As such, it is the very antithesis of the One energies. Whereas the One creates action without considering the consequences, the Two can be extremely sensitive, especially to the feelings of others. They are often paralysed into inaction by their imagined effect on others. It is the archetypal **feminine** number, ruled by the **moon**.

The Number 2 in relationships

The Number Two achieves its satisfaction and reward in life by creating harmony and balance in its home and world. Its role is not to succeed through willpower, force or domination, but to work through co-operation and diplomacy – its gifts are strongly focussed towards bringing others together and finding their common ground. They are the peacemakers of the world.

The more aggressive Number One often believes the Number Two is weak, subservient to others, easy-going and eager to please. In reality, the Number Two has great inner strengths, if it is able to reach them. While Number Ones can be shallow, Number Twos are quiet waters that run deep. Unfortunately, many Number Twos try to please others all the time, especially their partner and children, and can end up neglecting their own needs. This is the one area that Number Twos need to be aware of. They need to see that, by neglecting themselves, they stand a very good chance of reducing their effectiveness in the family by over-work, stress and the health problems this can create.

Number Twos assign blame readily when things go wrong. They can seem to be very judgmental, since they have a highly developed sense of responsibility – so much so that they can feel responsible

for anything and everything. It is the Number Twos who are quick to say 'Sorry' when someone bumps into them.

Many Number Twos feel a distinct lack of self-worth. Since they know deep down that they are the supporters and nurturers of the world, they may feel they are in the shadows all the time and can devalue themselves when they compare themselves with 'stronger' characters. It is easy for them to be timid, have their feelings easily hurt and worry unduly about what others may think or say. These Number Twos need to see that their consideration for others, endless patience and ability to see many sides of an issue are really strengths that many others lack. Without Number Twos around we would have anarchy.

The Number Two is often caught up in details, missing the big picture. If female, she may be pre-occupied with her 'ugly' nose and miss the fact that she is really very lovely. It can spoil her relationships, causing discord with her partner. The Number Two can be very fussy about their appearance and their home. They can have strong likes and dislikes and cling to their beliefs tenaciously, despite being shown facts to the contrary. Their challenge is to be open to change, despite their fears of being dominated by stronger characters.

In love, the Number Two is very popular. They need an intimate relationship for their happiness. They do not function very effectively without companionship, sympathetic understanding and love – in fact, they are most unhappy when alone or without love. They need a partner who has good taste and can share a charming home which is kept neat and clean. The Number Two can be a wonderful host/hostess and loves to have people around.

The Two hates standing out; it would rather be the 'power behind the throne'.

Key Energies:
- co-operative
- supportive
- sensitive
- tactful
- diplomatic

11

THE NUMBER 3

The Number Three deals with **synthesis.** It is the happy and joyful child emerging from the union of the Masculine One with the Feminine Two. The Number Three is youthful in appearance whatever the age and has a youthful outlook. It is full of enthusiasm and exuberance – a child of God. It inspires others and is a catalyst for turning the impossible into the possible. The Number Three is a dreamer and inspires others to turn these dreams into reality. It uses words to express itself. When a Three speaks, people should listen. Number Three is completion, a perfect balance of the duality of life. When the Three speaks from its heart, it is a channel from above. The Number Three is truly blessed. It is ruled by **Jupiter**.

The Number 3 in Relationships

The Number Three flourishes when its urge to create beauty is allowed full expression. A boring routine way of life is anathema to it, since it represents a limiting of its boundless creativity and need for spontaneity. If its enthusiasm is deadened, the Number Three becomes lifeless and unhappy. Partners need to avoid creating situations that either stifle, or do not support, the Three's abundant enthusiasm. Naturally, some of the Three's dreams can seem unrealistic to their partner, but it is unwise to underestimate the capabilities of the Three to make it all happen, provided it truly believes the vision.

The Number Three can do anything it sets its mind to and wants the very best that life has to offer. It attracts money without much effort or hard work. To others, the Three may seem lazy and lacking in application. No matter, when the Three believes in its great gift to attract what it wants, then it puts its imagination to work and hey presto! – there it is. That is the Three's major hurdle to jump – overcoming its often enormous self-doubt. This can be crippling to a very sensitive Three. Partners of Threes need to avoid criticism or withholding support.

The Number Three needs to be popular, to love and be loved. For without love, the Number Three is unhappy and feels no purpose in

life. It can love deeply, with affection and loyalty – sometimes giving with great self-sacrifice to those it loves.

The Number Three loves people, especially the opposite sex. In fact, the Three attracts the opposite sex in droves – it is aware of its attractiveness and really doesn't have to make much effort to attract partners. It would rather 'play the field' but is very loyal once it chooses its mate. Throughout its life, the Number Three may have many unusual romantic encounters, often starting out in a relationship in a very intimate way, especially sexually.

Because of its optimism, its desire for colour and beauty and its generous nature, the Number Three can be a most gracious, warm and loving partner. It requires a partner who can provide support and encouragement, for the Three can easily be discouraged because of its extreme sensitivity. The Number Three can swing from extreme confidence one moment ('I can do it') to the opposite the next moment ('How did I ever think I could do that?').

The Number Three prefers not to get its hands dirty, it would rather inspire and support others.

Key Energies:
- creative
- self-expressive
- gregarious
- self-doubt
- highly sensitive

The Number 4

The Number Four deals with **construction**. It is the number of building, of making ideas concrete and solid. It is the builder, the bringer of form and order to the world. It is deeply practical, turning raw materials into useful constructs and arranging them to fulfil a required plan. The Number Four is not an initiator but one who carries out the plans of others. It works within definite rules and regulations and keeps to the law. It loves pomp and ceremony, military parades, precision work of all types and routine. As such, it is the antithesis of the Number Three. It is ruled by the **Earth** and the **Sun**.

The Number 4 in Relationships

The Number Four is magnetically attracted to the Number One – they are both ruled by the Sun (Fours frequently live at Number One addresses). Whereas the Number One expresses the positive aspects of the Sun, the Four is decidedly negative. The Four looks up to the One and wishes it could be more dynamic, more free, more inspired, but the Number Four is firmly rooted to earthly concerns – security, money, possessions. Often, the Four finds life a grind, since they know they must earn their daily bread by the sweat of their brow. They believe they are born losers – often working long and hard for little reward, as they see it. Others, though, usually see the Number Four as being solid citizens, dependable, straightforward and a pillar of the community. Often, Fours can be rather complaining and see little joy in life.

The Number Four is basically serious-minded, especially about its family and enjoys family activities, simple pleasures, good wholesome food and a comfortable (not too stylish) home. It needs to feel secure within its relationship and prefers to be married than 'living together'. It believes strongly in tradition.

The Number Four, despite its need for order in its life, often becomes impatient and takes shortcuts. When it does, things fall apart and they have to start all over again. Fours need to learn they are here to build steadily, brick by brick, from the foundation up.

The Number Four holds very strong opinions of what is right and wrong. Partners need to be flexible with the sometimes bossy and opinionated Four. Its stubbornness is a result of needing to be in control of day-to-day operations – it hates being told what to do, and when and how to do it, without adequate consultation. If backed into a corner, the Number Four often becomes the 'Devil's advocate' and is suddenly argumentative and irritable. Partners need to understand that their Four needs to be consulted first to give it time to think about solutions, which it comes up with in its own time and in its own way. Partners need to take a roundabout approach with the Four.

Family (especially in-laws) is a major problem for the Number Four throughout its life. There is often some great opposition somewhere

within the family. Fours can then experience a battle of wills. Without respect for the Four's opinions, the Four can become resentful, feeling life is unfair and retreat into dark moods. The Number Four needs to see its duty as being there to provide a solid foundation for the protection and security of its family.

The Number Four usually makes money steadily rather than spectacularly and eventually gains financial security to a degree not attained by others of a more impulsive nature. It hates being hurried and moves slowly, sometimes painfully so. It misses many quick opportunities in life, but usually gets there in the end. Great patience is required from partners.

Number Fours are willing to help those in need, but their conservative and cautious nature limits their friends – an odd combination. Number Fours hold more contradictions than perhaps any other number.

The Number Four can make mountains out of molehills or can build something grand and worthwhile – their choice depends on their own self-image.

Key Energies:
- work
- worry
- practicality
- indecisive
- stable/unstable
- highly analytical

The Number 5

The Number Five deals with **human progress**. It exists to experience life fully – it is the administrator. It is ruled by **Mercury** and **Mars** – thus it is quick witted, mercurial, witty, enthusiastic and interested in the affairs of the world as well as having a spiritual leaning. It is the number of change (sometimes for its own sake), variety, travel and active involvement. Number Fives can work on the earthly plane as well as on spiritual planes. It is the number of the five senses of humankind, so is a very sensual number. It has a restless energy – always on the move with new projects, new places to explore, new people to meet forever lurking just beneath the surface. Their motto is: 'So many things to do – so little time'. They are freedom lovers and hate being cooped up. They are the free spirits and the eternal explorers, both physically and spiritually. They are the initiators of human progress.

The Number 5 in Relationships

The Number Five wrestles with its primary issue of **freedom** for most or all of its life. It has more emotional ups and downs than any other number. Against freedom is set **discipline** and this is the big bug-bear of most Fives. It is so easy for the Five to indulge in sensual pleasures and hedonistic activities and avoid taking personal responsibilities. It is usually prepared to cut and run when things get a little 'heavy' and 'boring' and yet it is here to exercise discipline, so that its responsibilities are balanced out. Flitting from one unfinished affair, project or job to another is a sure sign the Number Five is not gaining the depth of experience it really needs.

It needs to be reminded of the story of the well digger who, having dug well after well without hitting water, gave up without having his thirst quenched. If he had dug the first well a little deeper, he would have found water and saved himself a lot of trouble. So Fives need to stay with something past the point of boredom or frustration in order to break through to new levels of freedom that lie at deeper levels. This applies very much to their relationships. The simple, yet difficult secret for the Number Five is that only through discipline and focus can they achieve the grand freedom they so desire. **They need to realise that their feelings of being trapped is only a state of their mind**. Like the Number Three (which is twinned with the Five), it can be crippled by negative self-doubt, leading to dependency on others.

Number Fives, because they are interested in getting involved in a wide variety of activities, find themselves either spread too thin and facing burnout, or narrowly focussed on one idea. Either way, their health can suffer because of their obsessions. Number Fives can become great impostors, acting a variety of roles, until they discover

who they are. Their experiences can be very intense and short-lived as they move from one partner to another (often burning their bridges behind them), one career to another or one country to another. All this in the name of seeking a greater freedom in search, paradoxically, of a sense of identity through association (family, workmates, friends). The Number Five is a confusing character until it learns to focus on one relationship at a time. True **inner** freedom is then the reward.

The Number Five is the 'rolling stone that gathers no moss', but needs to put down roots to grow.

Key Energies:
- adventure
- involvement
- transcendence
- dependency
- easily bored

The Number 6

The Number Six deals with **unselfish loving service to others**. It is the provider and the caretaker of humanity. It is ruled by **Venus** and is a child of grace who lives to love. It has great personal appeal and loves its home. It works hard to give protection, security, happiness and abundance to its family and the world. It strives to make the world a far better place and doesn't hesitate to right all wrongs. It is a dreamer of how good things can be and is repelled by the crude, the nasty and the ungainly. It is a perfectionist, often fussing over minor details. Number Sixes are the visionaries, the futurists, who lead us towards a better future. They are 'home bodies' who like nothing more than having their family at home, all gathered around the fire.

The Number 6 in Relationships

The Number Six is here to reconcile their high vision of how things **should** be with how they actually are. In fact, the word 'should' figures prominently in their vocabulary. They are here, then, to expand their vision and learn to accept without constant judgment and criticism, for that is the trap many Sixes fall into in a big way. Most Number Sixes believe they are personally responsible for the perfect operation of the world (just as the Number Two does) and feel deep disappointment when things don't measure up to their often impossibly high standards. Many Sixes live in a constant state of desperation and disappointment until they learn to let their high ideals guide them, not rule them. Life for others in the home of such a Number Six parent can then be quite difficult, as no one can measure up in their eyes – people are either 'perfect' or 'flawed'.

When a Number Six meets someone for the first time, they enthuse: 'This person is perfect – just the person I have been waiting for', or they say 'This person is the pits', and has nothing more to do with them. There is no middle ground. Either the new person wears a halo or wears devil's horns. These extremist views inevitably sets up the poor Number Six for later disillusionment, as the new person's 'flaws' become apparent. Many Sixes are then torn between dropping the relationship, or living with it, since they have great loyalty and do not give up on anyone easily. These Sixes are capable of living the rest of their lives 'coping' with their lot, never truly expressing how they feel for fear of 'rocking the boat'. They carry the weight of the world on their drooping shoulders (body language gives them away).

Many Number Sixes spend a lot of their lives searching for the 'perfect' mate, 'perfect' house, 'perfect' situation (in common with the Number Nine). Partners of such Sixes cannot win. Only when the Six begins to appreciate its own inherent beauty will it stop criticising and appreciate others for who they are, instead of what they do or say.

The Number Six loves to love and be loved. Its life revolves around the family and children. Their urge is to protect their loved ones, regardless of whether this protection is welcome, so that they can easily smother them. This drives children and lovers away. Number Sixes need to be more sensitive to the real needs of their loved ones.

Key Energies:
- affectionate
- critical
- conservative
- stable

THE NUMBER 7

The Number Seven deals with **understanding**. It is forever asking questions, gathering information, examining plans in order to answer the eternal question: 'How and why does it work?' The Number Seven is separate from other humans – it is really a law unto itself. It operates outside the normal run of the mill situations. It is the thinker, the analyst. It is forever gathering knowledge, since for the Seven, knowledge is power – and the Seven is the first of the power numbers Seven, Eight and Nine. The Number Seven is ruled by **Neptune** and the **Moon**. Thus it is kept busy maintaining its often precarious balance between the material and the spiritual. Usually, the Seven goes one way or the other – either extremely materialistic or it is so very spiritual with no earthly concerns at all. Thus, most Number Sevens lead a pretty difficult life.

The Number 7 in Relationships

The Number Seven is basically a loner – the thinker (the famous statue by Rodin expresses the quintessential Seven energy) – and they are usually quite content to be on their own, rather than mix in with others. There is an air of the different about a Seven that sets them apart from all others. The Seven is often engaged in reflection and doesn't really want to be bothered with earthly concerns much. They like nothing more than tackling a problem where they can use their considerable powers of analysis and deduction. The Number Seven is the inventor, the scientist, the detective, and finds its path along a specialised line of work. It is often consulted for advice and delights in offering it.

The Number Seven generally finds relationships difficult, partners often becoming frustrated because of the reticence of the Seven and the reluctance to express itself. Very often, the Seven would rather die than express authentic feelings; provided, of course, it knows what these feelings actually are. Therein lies the difficulty for many Sevens. It is out of touch with its feelings – preferring instead to rationalise, to use logic, to communicate. Partners then do not know where they stand and communication dries up. Sevens need to appreciate how important it is to open up to an expression of their feelings – that feelings, especially tender ones, do not represent weakness. They often come across as being closed up emotionally. Intimate relationships cannot flourish under these conditions.

The Number Seven is usually not very flexible or adaptable in emotionally charged conditions. But, when it feels comfortable, it is a real 'gentlemen' or 'lady' and is the perfect companion. It can be very sceptical and suspicious and this leads to difficulties in relationships. Openness is the watchword for the Seven; it needs to understand others in greater depth in order to win the confidence it so desires from its partner.

The Seven doesn't like too many parties in its home – it loves small gatherings of people of like mind. It should choose a partner who also likes the finer things in life, seeks knowledge, is interested in books and who is of a similar intellectual level. Marrying into a large family can be difficult for a Seven, for it never feels comfortable in a family setting. A relationship based upon soul and mind attraction is the most satisfying for the Seven.

The Number Seven is the analyst and needs to be less suspicious and open up.

Key Energies:
- introspective
- secretive
- spiritual awareness or lack
- scholarship

THE NUMBER 8

The Number Eight deals with **judgment**. It is forever being placed in situations that require judgments to be made, authority to be exercised, power to be wielded and decisions made concerning itself and others 'under' it. It is ruled by **Saturn**, the planet of severity and limitation. Note the shape of the number eight. It is made up of two touching cyphers ('zeros') making up the 'infinity' sign standing on edge. It can be viewed as all or nothing and that sums up the energy of the Eight. It can be extremely ambitious to accumulate massive wealth (go for broke), but can self-destruct in the process. The Number Eight is intimately connected to the Number Four. It is second of the power numbers – the Eight wants power over others (the Seven wants power over self).

The Number 8 in Relationships

The Number Eight is forever busy – always on the go. Often it has a manic intensity which can destroy the very thing it is striving for. It is the most self-destructive number, unless it learns to take time out, to relax, and to slow down. It is a strong personality, often a domineering one. It gets on well with others and shows a strong interest in others, particularly if they are important, are wealthy or are at the top of their company or profession.

There is very often a strange contradiction in the Number Eight. It is driven by high ambition and a great sense of purpose. It can focus on a plan, a business idea or venture with great intensity, often supervising others brilliantly. However, just when success is at hand, it can get an attack of nerves and either fail to follow through to success or allow another to claim credit. It seems to have a love-hate relationship with success and money. Many Eights spend their lives attempting to remove the responsibilities of dealing with money or worldy acclaim and success.

It loves big houses, big cars, expensive clothes – all the trappings of 'success', for the Eight is a very materialistic number. It doesn't like to give much without the promise of an immediate return. If male, he often wears big jewellery and a big watch. If female, she often wears 'power' clothes for business.

The Number Eight rises to the top in everything or, at least, wants to. It often speaks with bluntness and does not 'suffer fools gladly', It can show bursts of temper when frustrated by the inadequate efforts of others but its anger soon subsides.

In love, the Number Eight is loyal and devoted. But with so many plans churning around in its mind, it can have little time for romance, despite being in love. It needs to learn to slow down and take time to express love and beauty. Partners of Eights need to be self-sufficient and to accept that their Number Eight's world revolves around their work.

The Number Eight wants everything – and wants it NOW.

Key Energies:
- ambitious
- successful
- self-destructive
- opportunistic
- philanthropic

THE NUMBER 9

The Number Nine completes the cycle of Root Numbers and deals with **wisdom and forgiveness.** It is here to live with integrity and in tune with its higher intuition, having learned all the previous eight lessons (in previous lifetimes). When it does, it inspires others to greatness. It is a leader (as is the Number One) but, whereas the One leads by force of will, the Nine leads by example. Whereas the One is concerned only with self, the Nine is concerned with the world. Nines need to understand that what they say, think or do can have a great impact on others. For the Nine has considerable charisma and tends to draw others to itself. It is ruled by **Uranus.** It uses the world as its canvas and wants so desperately to make the world a better place. Often, it has gained its wisdom from losses and

major disappointments in its life and so is an emotionally charged number. However, the Nine is divinely protected and is a 'survivor'.

The Number 9 in Relationships

The Number Nine is a most charming individual – its sympathy for others, its warmth of feeling, its interest in the affairs of others makes it well liked and generally a good companion. Many Nines have had a severe loss early in its life (a close family member dying, for instance) and has experienced deep sorrow. This gives the Nine a highly developed sense of compassion.

The Number Nine loves its home, family and friends. It loves beauty in people and objects. It is very idealistic and often spends its life searching for that 'perfect' mate, which always eludes it. It falls in love quickly and with great intensity, but can fall out of love just as quickly if it find its mate doesn't live up to the impossibly high ideals it has first set. It has many romances and friendships until it realises that the 'perfect' love it is seeking is the reward for altruistic service and a life based on the higher spiritual principles.

Most Number Nines struggle to live in accord with their highest principles – they often bend the rules, especially spiritual laws, since they find great difficulty in accepting responsibility for their thoughts and actions. They often fool themselves that it doesn't matter what they think or do, so long as they 'keep their noses clean'. These Nines haven't yet realised that being born with the highest vibration or energy they, above all other numbers, are being asked to live with the highest personal integrity and honesty. This means they must be a shining example for others. Anything less than this will result in a life of struggle, division and severe loss.

One way to live with integrity is to 'practise what you preach'. Here is where many Nines go astray – because they tend to live 'in their heads', their powerful logical minds often override the true messages that their intuition is providing. They tend to rationalise their thoughts and actions. Their hearts may be telling them to do one thing (often it goes against established custom), but their heads may be telling them to play it safe, swim with the tide, don't take any risks.

The result can often be missed opportunities and a sense of regret that may last their whole life. Those Number Nines in tune with their inner wisdom radiate considerable magnetism.

Many Nines still searching for life's meaning are attracted to charismatic 'gurus' or religious movements, since Nines are usually very impressionable. They believe that someone out there holds the key to their deepest questions. These Nines move from one guru or teaching to another in search of their 'Holy Grail'. They need to recognise that the answers lie within. They need to learn to take full responsibility for their lives, since many Number Nines ignore basic spiritual and Karmic laws (the law of cause and effect). They may then feel burdened and a 'victim' of someone else's actions. They fail to see the part they played in this drama and feel as if they are being 'punished', especially if their self-esteem is already very low.

In their relationships, Nines need to continually keep asking the question: 'What is the generous, compassionate, bold choice I must make here?' Too often, Nines rely heavily on the opinions of others, especially people who have strong, opinionated personalities. But there is a paradox with Nines – those Nines that rely heavily on others' opinions will themselves act as though their own opinions are 'written on tablets of stone'. These Nines need to become more flexible in their approach and to admit there is no absolute truth.

The Nine may choose between 'hiding its light under a bushel', or being a shining beacon for all to follow.

Key Energies:
- highly emotional
- humanitarian
- leader
- fanatic
- compassion
- forgiveness

The above nine numbers represent the nine fundamental energies of human existence. All other numbers derive from these roots. Let's now look at the special Compound Numbers – the Master Numbers Eleven and Twenty-Two.

THE MASTER NUMBERS 11 AND 22

There is much disagreement among numerologists about the meaning of the Master Numbers. Most would agree, though, that anyone working one of the Master Numbers is being asked to live their life on an extremely high vibration and has a special role to play, *provided they live up to their potential*. One word – the name 'Master Number' doesn't necessarily mean that the person is a master of anything. Anyone working their particular number, whatever it is, at a very high level is a 'master'.

Those working the Number Eleven must first pass through the trials and tribulations of the Two (Eleven reduces to the root Two) – issues of balance, self-assertion, creative co-operation. Therefore, early in life, many Elevens need to discover themselves, to learn to uncover and use their willpower. The Number Eleven consists of two Ones and so is endowed with a double dose of will (see the Number One section above). With the force of the One, combined with the inner strengths of the Two, the Number Eleven is a leader. A strong personal ambition turns the Eleven into a leader towards darkness (Hitler had Eleven prominent in his chart). However, with love in its heart, the Eleven is a 'bringer of the light' into people's lives.

Key Energies:
● the Two keeps the home fires burning
● the Eleven goes out into the world and lights the fires

Those working the very high Twenty-Two vibration must first pass through the issues of the Number Four (Twenty-Two reduces to the root Four) – issues of practicality, making plans real and building its life up steadily step by step (read the section on the Number Four earlier on). When 'firing on all cylinders', the Twenty-Two has child-like innocence and goes out into the world sharing its great wisdom and love.

Key Energies:
● the Four takes the world to heart
● the Twenty-Two takes heart to the world

We have covered the Root Numbers and the Master Numbers. What about the Compound Numbers 10, 12, 13, ...? The primary energy of these numbers is given by the associated Root Number. For instance, the Compound Number 18 has the primary energy of the Root 1 + 8 = **9**, with the added flavour of the 1 and the 8 energies. For further discussion of Compound Numbers, refer to *Numerology for Beginners* by Kristyna Arcarti in this series.

The numerical value of the letters of the alphabet

In modern numerology, we take the 'English' alphabet and assign a numerical value to it according to its place in the alphabet. Thus, A = 1, B = 2, C = 3, etc.

TABLE 1

A – 1	J – 1	S – 1
B – 2	K – 2	T – 2
C – 3	L – 3	U – 3
D – 4	M – 4	V – 4
E – 5	N – 5	W – 5
F – 6	O – 6	X – 6
G – 7	P – 7	Y – 7
H – 8	Q – 8	Z – 8
I – 9	R – 9	

Why not copy this chart and keep it with you? You will soon remember the values of all the letters and be able to analyse names quickly. Refer to the exercise in the Introduction where you worked out your family name number. Now gain some practice by working out the numbers of your friends, relatives, workmates.

The Karmic Numbers Sixteen and Nineteen

As was mentioned before, **not all numbers are benevolent**. Sixteen is an unfortunate number, while nineteen is very fortunate.

The **Number Sixteen** is associated with sudden accidents, losses and catastrophes. The Numbers One and Six are both materialistic and when combined, produce Seven, a highly spiritual number. When the One and the Six come together, they live on materialistic planes and reject any intrusion of Spirit into their lives. Only when they get 'wake-up calls' of suffering losses and 'accidents' will they realise that Spirit needs to be incorporated into their lives for their real happiness.

Most people born on the sixteenth of any month will begin their lives striving for wealth, for financial security, for high position. With continued striving, their health usually suffers, or they suffer financial losses, a divorce and their world falls apart. Then, they are given an open space where they can rebuild their life from a more spiritual base. Will they use their innate wisdom (from the Seven) and take this opportunity?

The **Number Nineteen** is a very fortunate number. It is associated with spiritual rebirth. The One and the Nine combine to produce Ten, which is a rebirth of One ($1 + 9 = 10$; $1 + 0 = 1$). The will of the One combines positively with the humanity of the Nine. The number Nineteen is being asked to stand on its own two feet and take courage to begin the journey of self-development, self-enlightenment. Most people born on the nineteenth of any month have a sunny disposition and look at life on the bright side, eagerly enjoying life's challenges and changes.

YOUR LIFE PATH AND LIFE PURPOSE NUMBERS

Discover your Life Path and Life Purpose from your birthdate

Now that we have understanding of the symbology of numbers and letters, let us apply our knowledge to uncovering how we function. **Our Life Path and Life Purpose numbers are derived entirely from our date of birth**. If you think about it, this is a most remarkable discovery. Just as astrology can predict one's character from the time, date and place of birth so can numerology, but from date of birth only.

Just think – on the day you were born, an imprint is made of your character assets which will help you through life, your talents, abilities and your heritage from the past – all recorded in the date of your birth. If you have children, you can reduce their anxieties and difficulties in growing up by using this knowledge wisely. **You will know exactly how to guide and encourage them individually towards their destiny – and you will know a great deal about their destiny**. Armed with these insights, you will find greater meaning as a parent.

Your Life Path is the route by which you accomplish your Life Purpose or your Destiny. Some people have compatible numbers on their Life Path and Life Purpose, while others have difficult combinations.

Your Life Purpose – Why are you here?

You may be amazed to learn that the question of what you are here to accomplish on earth (your **Life Purpose**) is contained in your **date of birth**. That is the 'secret' (esoteric) knowledge contained in the numbers you carry with you throughout your entire life. And the way you accomplish your tasks (your **Life Path**) is contained in the **day of the month** on which you were born.

Three steps to discover your Life Purpose

Your **Life Purpose** is taken from your **complete date of birth** (day, month and year). If you were born on 4 January 1953, we can work out your Life Purpose as follows:

> 4   January   1953

STEP 1 – Write the digits of the day, month and year of birth down:

> 4   1   1953 (don't forget to include the '19--')

STEP 2 – Now add up all the digits:

> $4 + 1 + 1 + 9 + 5 + 3 = 23$

Your Life Purpose is **23**, which is a Compound Number.

STEP 3 – Reduce the 23 to a Root Number. Add the 2 to the 3 to obtain the Root, and we get **5**. Your Life Purpose is **5**. It's that simple.

Next we can do another Life Purpose for someone born on 24 November 1965. We write day, month and year as before:

> 24   November   1965

STEP 1 – We write as:

> 24   11   1965

STEP 2 – Add all the digits:

$$2 + 4 + 1 + 1 + 1 + 9 + 6 + 5 = 29.$$

Your Life Purpose is **29**, which is a Compound Number.

STEP 3 – Reduce the 29 to a Root Number. Add the 2 to the 9 and we get **11**. This is a **Master Number**, so first go to the Root Number (in this case $1 + 1 = 2$), refer to it in Chapter 1, then read about the Master Number **11**.

HINTS: a) Make sure you use the correct number for the month:

1	January	5	May	9	September
2	February	6	June	10	October
3	March	7	July	11	November
4	April	8	August	12	December

b) When a ten, twenty or thirty appears, for instance the birthdate 20 October 1938, always write all individual digits as follows: $2 + 0 + 1 + 0 + 1 + 9 + 3 + 8 = \mathbf{24}$. It is incorrect to write the ten and twenty as: $20 + 10 + 1 + 9 + 3 + 8 = \mathbf{51}$.

c) Write the final Life Path and Life Purpose numbers using a slash mark, as follows: Say the Life Path is **24** and Life Purpose is **23**. To indicate the root numbers, write the root to the right of the slash mark: Life Path is **24/6** and Life Purpose **23/5**. **The Root Number to the right of the slash mark is always the sum of the two numbers to the left.**

d) Double-check your addition.

EXERCISE

Look at the Life Paths and Purposes for the following birthdates:

		Write digits here	Life Path	Life Purpose
1	18 July 1976	$1+8+7+1+9+7+6 = 39$	**18/9**	$39 = \mathbf{12/3}$
2	9 January 1906	$9+1+1+9+0+6 = 26$	**9**	**26/8**
3	30 March 1899	$3+0+3+1+8+9+9 = 33$	**30/3**	**33/6**

Now do these yourself: (Answers at the end of this Chapter)

4 29 September 1949 ....

5 3 March 1995 ....

6 24 March 1994 ....

7 23 August 1940 ....

8 10 December 1953 ....

9 19 May 1980 ....

10 25 April 1979 ....

Your personal Life Path and Life Purpose

Now let's work out your Personal Life Path and Life Purpose Numbers.

STEP 1 – Write down the day, month and year of your birth:

....   19......

(day)   (month)   (year)

STEP 2 – Add up all the digits and write the total here:

+   +   +   +   +   +   + = ...

STEP 3 – From the total obtained in Step 2, write down the total as a Compound Number to the left of the slash mark. Then add up the individual digits making up the total to obtain the Root Number:

....../ ......   **This number is your Life Purpose
Numbers**.

Write here the **day of the month** on which you were born:

....

If this number is a Compound Number, write the Root Number to the right of the slash mark:

........./ ......   **The Root Number is your Life Path.**

These are the most important numbers to describe your role in life.

31

Your energies and issues revealed

Now you know your Life Path and Life Purpose numbers, check against the Key Energies and issues for your numbers: Refer to Chapter 1 for background detail on each of your numbers and then proceed to read about the number below.

The number 1 life path and life purpose

Many Ones are born into a family where one or both parents are domineering and overpowering (more often than not, it is the opposite sex parent who is most unyielding). This tends to crush the fragile confidence of the One early in life, which creates much tension and conflict in the home until the child reaches its teens, where it goes through a period of intense rebellion. Often, the One finds life at home intolerable and leaves. For years thereafter, the One will feel as if its life is a battle against the whole world and it feels alone. Extreme independence is the watchword. All relationships in this period are fraught with power struggles and are usually short-lived.

As the One matures, it begins to value individuality and self-will in others. It then, begins to actively cooperate with others from a more secure foundation and develop firmer relationships. Many Ones, who have not worked out the struggles between their will and the wills of others, will often attract a partner who is just as wilful and obstinate (a 'substitute' for their domineering parent). Many Number Ones live in a state of exasperation with their partner for years before they 'spread their wings' and take courage and do their own thing.

Ones can accelerate this learning process by seeing that the obstinacy and willfulness in others is just a reflection of those very traits in themselves. They can harmonise their lives by agreeing to submit to the greater will, rather than their own ego's needs. Seeing the 'big picture' of humanity is the Number One's greatest challenge.

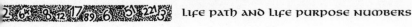
LIFE PATH AND LIFE PURPOSE NUMBERS

Some fortunate Number Ones are born into supportive families that fosters self-esteem of all members. These Ones can enter into relationships secure in themselves and supportive of their partner, whose individuality is loved and supported by the One.

The Number One's Life Purpose is to develop its creativity and self-confidence in positive ways.

THE NUMBER 2 LIFE PATH AND LIFE PURPOSE

Many Twos are born into a family where parents are petty minded, critical and contrary. The child isn't complimented or encouraged much – instead, they are constantly told they could have done better. Whatever the child does, it is never good enough. Of course, this damages the child's self-confidence and the Two withdraws into the child's shell, sometimes for many years. It is often unable to make decisions on its own for fear of being 'wrong' and thereby criticised.

In early relationships, many Twos take a back seat and 'play second fiddle'. They are thus vulnerable to domination and are quite often abused mentally and physically. Then, these Twos retreat into repressed or expressed feelings of frustration and resentment and will often take it out on weaker individuals. The Number Two needs to realise that if they are in such a position in a relationship, they need to release judgments of others, self-righteousness and critical attitudes in order to bring out their natural ability to move forward through persuasion rather than by brute force.

When Number Twos are working at or near their full potential, they are loving, supportive and well-balanced people. They live for their relationships with their loved ones. They know where to balance giving with taking and are fair but firm with their children. They know where to draw the line between what is their own responsibility and that of the other person. They are stable and dependable with a very large warm homely energy.

The Number Two's Life Purpose is to learn to co-operate with others and achieve balance in its life.

33

THE NUMBER 3 LIFE PATH AND LIFE PURPOSE

The Number Three is life itself – forever youthful, forever fertile, forever seeking new forms of expression in a beautiful way. Many Threes are therefore born into families where their self-expression and artistic creativity are stifled, if not crushed entirely (but not permanently). Because the Three is fertility personified, it has a highly sexual (and sensual) nature, which it often suppresses early in life because of parents who may not allow any show of affection or sexuality in the house. This creates much confusion for the young Three, who then feels guilt and shame in early sexual encounters. The Three often awakens sexually much later than its peers.

The young Three is a very sensitive creature who is easily hurt. It can therefore develop a hard skin and retreat into itself and live on its intellect. Only when the Three learns to rid itself of the fear of openly expressing its feelings and using its highly developed intuition, can the Three enter into warm, loving relationships. This may take years to develop, especially when unsupportive parents are involved.

The Three usually enters into love relationships full of enthusiasm and giving its all. With the Three, a partner certainly gets full 'value for money'. Very often, the relationship starts off very intensely sexually with the Three going in 'head over heels'. But, if the Three's interest in its partner begins to waver, it can fall 'out of love' very quickly and wonder how it became involved with that partner in the first place. Threes can enter and end a relationship in record time. The Three needs to feel that the relationship is growing and developing to maintain its interest. Partners of Threes need to keep the emotional pot bubbling to avoid stagnation.

The Number Three's Life Purpose is to develop its self-expressive powers with sensitivity and honesty.

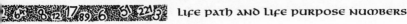

THE NUMBER 4 LIFE PATH AND LIFE PURPOSE

The Four is a practical type, not normally given to a romantic approach to love. It is usually ruled by its head, not its heart. It likes to have all the facts before making a move and takes few risky chances. It has a strong sense of right and wrong and strong likes and dislikes. Despite this, the Four is naturally friendly and approachable, if very selective, in its relationships.

Very often, the Four has experienced hardship in its early life and has had to work to help support the family. Because of these experiences the Four, later in life, continues to see difficulties everywhere.

The Number Four can be quite inflexible in love and doesn't like surprises. It can be very ardent, but with passions well under control. It needs to plan everything out, sometimes down to the last detail. It is not adventurous but can be the salt of the earth; dependable and sensible. Partners who are more spontaneous (especially if they are Number Three or Five) need to slow down and patiently allow the Four to consider the various options on its own before making decisions.

Above all, the Four loves praise from its partner for a job well done. But woe betide anyone who gives less than their best – the Four can be scathing in its criticism (while ignoring its own deficiencies).

The Number Four's Life Purpose is to create stability in its life through steady application.

THE NUMBER 5 LIFE PATH AND LIFE PURPOSE

The Number Five is surrounded by an aura of change, restlessness, sensuality, freedom and curiosity of the world. Whether the Five chooses to wander the earth in its quest or to stifle its natural impulse for constant variety in its life depends on many factors – the Five can easily go both ways. Many adventurous Fives are born to parents who actively discourage its need to explore life (see the Number One Life Path and Purpose for a similar pattern). The Five child will feel insecure and often falls into the infantile habit of repeating the same mistake over and over. This applies very much to early relationships. Fives can have a succession of partners who are remarkably similar as they resist the opportunity to learn from each one.

The Five needs a partner who is just as flexible, quick-witted, flirtatious and fun-loving. The Five does not like a partner who is a challenge to its popularity (the Five, remember, is ruled by Mercury and Mars). The Five likes to help others, even when help is not requested and it can be overbearing, knowing what is 'best' for its partner. It can thus create friction at home.

The Five loves outdoor pursuits and sports with its mate. As for its home life, it is not easy for the Five to adjust to the routine of family demands but, given sufficient latitude, the Five can enjoy its family and gives a lot when it is around.

The Five needs to know how its partner is feeling – it is itself an emotional individual and avoids emotional conflicts whenever possible. It can get the emotions stirred up in the home and then depart the scene. On its return, it is often surprised that its partner is still hurt; the Five having forgotten all about the incident.

The Number Five's Life Purpose is to experience freedom through a disciplined approach to life.

THE NUMBER 6 LIFE PATH AND LIFE PURPOSE

The Number Six is the most domestic and home loving of all the numbers. It lives primarily to serve others, especially its immediate family. Whenever someone comes to it in need, it drops everything, goes to the rescue and is always ready with a shoulder for someone to cry on or a nourishing meal. The Six is capable of considerable sacrifice and it can remind its loved ones of this sacrifice when it is unhappy.

The Number Six enjoys its home comforts and rarely prefers travel to staying at home. It enjoys harmonious surroundings, although it doesn't need luxury to be content. It is often a complete 'fuss pot' in the home, where everything has to be in its right place. Nothing can be allowed to spoil the domestic order so life for a partner who is more flexible and casual in its way of living, can be difficult.

One of life's difficulties for Sixes is that they are unable to 'see the wood for the trees'. Their vision of life is then restricted to the mundane and the ordinary. Because of their idealism and tendency to be judgmental these Sixes become moody and discouraged. They can then lash out angrily, especially at their partner if the Six does not receive the affection and concern that it believes is its due.

The Number Six's Life Purpose is to open up its view of life and learn to accept that perfection is always present.

TḄE NUMBER 7 LIFE PATḄ AND LIFE PURPOSE

The Seven is aloof, reserved, separate, intellectual, studious and detached. It carries great wisdom which it delights in displaying to others, often boring them in the process. It is, like the Six, very judgmental and stern and has strong opinions about what other people are doing. It is honest and logical, though it cannot be budged from its asserted positions.

In emotional situations, the Seven is most uncomfortable and will 'switch off'. It finds it difficult, if not impossible, to be tender and say loving words to its partner. It approaches romance in a serious way, as intellectual rapport with its partner is uppermost for the Seven. When trust for its partner has been established, the Seven can be loyal and possess long lasting deep feelings for its mate.

The Seven can be a difficult love partner because of its tendency to withdraw into its shell when the emotional heat is turned up. It then switches into its rational mode and communication dries up. Maintaining its poise and self-control is all important for the Seven and as an emotional outburst would definitely upset the apple cart, it avoids them like the plague.

The Number Seven's Life Purpose is to intuitively trust their inner wisdom and to open themselves up emotionally to others.

The NUMBER 8 Life path AND Life purpose

The Number Eight is all about power and its accumulation and exercise. It loves to be the leader in a competitive situation and it loves to win. It is a powerful personality and attracts respect. It likes to get things done and isn't overly concerned about the sensibilities of others, just as long as the result is good. It isn't given to fine points of meaning since it is, above all, a materialistic individual.

In love, it is like the Seven in that it tends to hide its deeper emotions and become detached. It hesitates to show any form of tenderness, since it believes that would demonstrate weakness and it would then be vulnerable to domination, which it abhors. Because it is able to see through the needs of its partner quite readily, it can be manipulative.

It is proud and if motivated by personal gain, it can use others shamelessly. For these Eights, acquiring personal wealth and power out of greed will usually result in great loss and sudden setbacks. This experience forces the Eight to look at its motives. When harmony is established, the Eight can 'go for gold' and do much good for itself, its family, and the world. Always, the Eight must have a goal to shoot for, even in leisure pursuits, for it thrives on competition.

The Eight seeks an able partner, one who accomplishes much in his or her own right. They enjoy all the trappings of the 'good life' and accumulate the major status symbols to indicate to others their material success.

The Number Eight's Life Purpose is to live harmoniously with abundance and to exercise power wisely.

THE NUMBER 9 LIFE PATH AND LIFE PURPOSE

As the final Root Number with the highest vibration, the Number Nine is the idealist. It dreams of the perfect world, the perfect career, the perfect partner. It lives in an inner world of dreams and ideas and sees its role in life as the wise counsel. However, it is not just a dreamer – it is a doer as well, although its actions are not business-oriented, and it has a mystical air that many are drawn to.

Possessing extreme emotional sensitivity, the Nine can fluctuate between moodiness and depression when things do not work out, to elation when they do, especially in relationships. They can take life too seriously and become reclusive, hiding themselves away from the imperfect world out there. When awakened, the Nine is a shining light for others, radiating charisma and magnetism, for they are here to serve humanity.

Of all the numbers, the Nine has perhaps the greatest difficulty with relationships. This is not because the 'fates are against them', but that their ideals can be impossibly high, and they search the world (sometimes literally) looking for that perfect partner and situation. They can be excited by the exotic, or the unreachable (already married partners) and often have long-distance relationships, which can self-destruct when they begin living together. For these Nines, the fantasy is more exciting than the reality.

The Nine's Life Path and Purpose is to live with total integrity allowing their innate wisdom to reach far and wide.

Now we have examined the nine Root Numbers, let us now take a look at the Master Numbers, Eleven and Twenty-Two.

THE NUMBER 11 LIFE PATH AND LIFE PURPOSE

You should refer to the description of the Two energies in Chapter 1, since the basic Eleven energy is Two (1 + 1 = **2**). With the two Ones, the Eleven's issues are all about confidence and creativity (a double dose!), but with the desire to serve humanity and bring peace to the world. The Eleven, therefore, usually has a strong drive and ambition, which moves it up into positions of considerable influence and public prominence. If tempted by a motive of personal gain rather than altruism, the Eleven may get things done, but is seldom loved.

The Eleven, because of its idealism, may be drawn into movements with visionary aims. They can become fanatical about a cause or their work. If so, the Eleven can easily be out of touch with the needs of those around them, and can ride roughshod over their sensitivities while in relentless pursuit of their own goals. Towards those without 'fire in their bellies', the Eleven can be a bully and can overpower more timid souls.

With the conflicting combination of great loyalty and diplomacy set against their independent streak, Elevens usually have eventful and dramatic relationships. In fact their whole lives can appear to be a complete paradox. Sexually many Elevens, who have abundant energy anyway, swing between frequent sexual activity and total abstention. It's as if there are two opposing characters inside the body of the Eleven.

The Eleven's Life Purpose is to strike a harmonious balance in its own life so as to bring harmony to the world.

THE NUMBER 22 LIFE PATH AND LIFE PURPOSE

The Twenty-Two's life unfolds similarly to the Four (2 + 2 = **4**), so you should read about the Four in Chapter One. The Twenty-Two

has a great need to organise things through cooperation and tactful diplomacy. They are generally not leaders, but are often seen quietly working behind the scenes, keeping everything together and gradually building up the organisation or venture.

Most Twenty-Twos use the relationships with their parents and siblings in early home life as the foundation for their future relationships – much more so than for any other number. To fully function, they need to clear up any blocked energies they have with their family, since a blockage here looms very large in their lives. Also, in common with many other Fours, the Twenty-Two often has experienced some form of childhood abuse which needs to be dealt with before sexual expression is possible.

As Twenty-Twos mature, they move away from thinking and doing what others expect of them towards an over-reaction, where they become unconventional and non-conformist. As with all Two energies, they need to avoid extremes and get their lives in balance.

Twenty-Twos have wonderful analytical powers and are able to build large organisations. They can tend to overanalyse and worry compulsively. When this happens they become stuck and, to move forward, they often make rash decisions which they later regret.

The Number Twenty-Two's Life Purpose is to prepare the foundations for the future of humanity by bringing others together, inspiring them with their vision.

Case study – The Late Diana, Princess of Wales

As a very high-profile figure, the late Diana, Princess of Wales is a wonderful subject for numerology analysis. She was born on 1 July, 1961. So we know, from the day of the month of her birth, that she had a Life Path of the Number One.

What does this number represent? It is the number of the leader, the one in control (or needing to be in control), the creator. As we

41

discovered, the One Life Path often experiences early conflicts at home with parents. Perhaps her chronic shyness in youth stemmed from having her self-confidence undermined.

Later in life she began to find her sense of independence and took the initiative, supporting many charities and humanitarian causes in her own right, apart from her royal status. She seemed to have had little support from the Establishment, as she 'went where angels feared to tread'. Her much publicised battle with bulimia was a major issue over control.

When she married Prince Charles, she was partnered with a man who was stubborn, obstinate and unyielding, as she herself was. There seemed to be a constant battle of wills as they fought for supremacy. Their marriage could not last with such conflicts. She appeared to be the model 'bird in a gilded cage' – a classic Number One situation.

Compare Diana's life with description of the One energies outlined in Chapters 1 and 2.

Does her life fit the Number One Path?

Now let's look at her Life Purpose …

Write her birthday:	1	July	1961
	1	7	1961

Now add the digits:

Life Purpose ……… 25/7

Now we know Diana's Life Purpose was Seven. Refer to Chapters 1 and 2 for a description of those energies.

Above all, the main characteristic of the Seven is as a loner, someone who values its privacy and guards it jealously. This certainly applied to Diana who, in death, appeared to many as a person apart with a considerable spiritual dimension. The major purpose for the Seven is to learn to trust their intuition **and to communicate their wisdom to others**. Towards the end of her life, Diana was certainly coming out of her shell, touching the lives of more and more people and living the Seven energy.

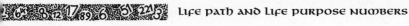

Compare Diana's life with the description of the Seven energies. Does her life fit the Number Seven Life Path?

EXERCISE

The LIfe path aND LIfe puRpose of youR faMILy

Now work out the Life Path and Life Purpose numbers and energies from birthdates for your family and friends.

	Date of Birth	Life Path	Life Purpose
Yourself	....	.. /..	.../..
Your partner	....	.. /..	.../..
Mother	....	.. /..	.../..
Father	....	.. /..	.../..
Brother	....	.. /..	.../..
Sister	....	.. /..	.../..
Aunt	....	.. /..	.../..
Uncle	....	.. /..	.../..
Friend	....	.. /..	.../..
Work colleague	....	.. /..	.../..
Other	....	.. /..	.../..
Other	....	.. /..	.../..

Answers to exercise on p.30:

Birthdate	Life Path	Life Purpose
29 September 1949	29/11	43/7
3 March 1995	3	30/3
26 March 1994	26/8	34/7
23 August 1940	23/5	27/9
10 December 1953	10/1	22/4
19 May 1980	19/1	33/6
25 April 1979	25/7	37/1

DISCOVER YOURSELF AND YOUR PARTNER FROM YOUR BIRTH NAME

As we found in the Introduction and Chapter 1, your name holds the secret to your personality, your inner desires and your spiritual mission. Refering to Table 1 (see p.26), let's do an example:

Take the birth name **Sarah Elizabeth Moore**. We work with birth names, since this name reflects you at birth. Later changes to your name (say, by marriage) will have an effect, but what you are born with will stay with you all your life.

Separate the consonants from the vowels, writing the value of the vowels *above* the name, and the value of the consonants *below* the name. Then, add the value of the consonants, then the value of the vowels and then the value of the full name. These three numbers comprise the main features of Sarah's personality, as she expresses herself in the world.

THE SOUL URGE, PERSONALITY AND EXPRESSION NUMBERS

1 The sum total of the vowels we call her **Soul Urge** (her inner longings)

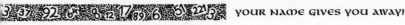

2   The sum total of the consonants we call her **Personality** (how she is seen by others)
3   The sum total of all letters we call her **Expression** (what she must do in life).

```
      1   1      5   9   1   5            6   6    5  = 39 = 3 = SOUL URGE
    S A R A H    E L I Z A B E T H    M O O R E
    1   9   8      3   8   2   2   8      4      9    = 54 = 9 = PERSONALITY
                                              Total  93 = 3 = EXPRESSION
```

We see that Sarah shows a **9 Personality** (humanitarian, highly emotional), has a **Soul Urge** of **3** (needs to find the romance and beauty in life), with an **Expression** of **3** (artistic, kind, inspirational).

Soul Urge

Why are the vowels (a, e, i, o, u, plus y) associated with the soul? Think of how the vowels are produced by the body. All vowel sounds are made by gently forcing air from the deepest part of the lungs through the vocal cords and out of the open mouth. Consonants sounds are made by movements of the tongue, lips and teeth, with many of the sounds made by a violent expelling of air past just opened lips.

Thus, the vowels come from deep within (the soul), while the consonants come from closer to the surface (the personality).

Your Soul Urge represents your deepest desires in life. It is one of the most important numbers you have. Sometimes, it is well hidden for many years but it is our destiny to be true to our Soul Urge.

Personality

This is given by the sum total of the consonants of your birth name. It is how others see you. It is through your personality that you express yourself to others. It is not the true self but should be the channel through which your true character is expressed.

EXPRESSION

This is given by the sum total of all the letters in your birth name. It represents that which you must do in life, despite your protestations. It is the spiritual mission you must accept. Many of your setbacks in life are a result of the tests that this number has made upon you. It is often a difficult task meeting this requirement, but keeping an eye on the goal will result in accomplishment and an invigorating feeling which comes from having a definite sense of purpose.

When you know what your name means, you have had a major spiritual awakening.

EXERCISE

WORK OUT THE SOUL URGE, PERSONALITY, AND EXPRESSION FOR YOURSELF, YOUR PARENTS, YOUR CHILDREN, AND YOUR PARTNER OR FRIEND.

Write the numbers here, remembering to reduce all Compound double-digit Numbers to their Root, except the Master Numbers 11 and 22. Refer to the sections in this book on what each number means. Do you have the same number on a particular position as another member of your family? If so, do you feel a special connection?

	Soul Urge	Personality	Expression
Yourself	....	....	....
Partner	....	....	....
Mother	....	....	....
Father	....	....	....
Brother	....	....	....
Sister	....	....	....
Son	....	....	....
Daughter	....	....	....
Other	....	....	....
Other	....	....	....

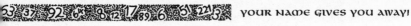

As we found in the Introduction, your family name (surname) has an important bearing on you, as does your first name and any middle name. Your first or given name is the personal side of your nature and shows personal attitudes and feelings. Your middle name(s) is a support from which hidden reserves of strength can be drawn, while your surname has a strong inherited family background and has great influence in your life.

So let us examine Sarah's names separately, adding the vowels and consonants for each name in turn:

	Soul Urge	Personality	Expression
Sarah	2	9	2
Elizabeth	2	5	7
Moore	8	4	3
Full name	3	9	3

We see that Sarah will have difficulties reconciling her inherited need for spontaneity and joy with a rather laid-back approach (the 3 Expression of the Moore name) with the strong feelings of duty to others of the 2 Soul Urge and Expression of the Sarah name. Luckily, she has the wise 7 in the Elizabeth Expression.

EXERCISE

WORK OUT THE SOUL URGE, THE PERSONALITY AND EXPRESSION NUMBERS OF YOUR NAME AND YOUR PARTNER'S NAME

Compare your numbers in the chart below. Can you spot any correspondences? Are there the same numbers on the same positions or in different positions? Remember to use your birth names.

	Soul Urge	Personality	Expression
Mine–Partner's first name	....–....	....–....	....–....
Mine–Partner's second name	....–....	....–....	....–....
Mine–Partner's family name	....–....	....–....	....–....
Mine–Partner's full name	....–....	....–....	....–....

If you and your partner have the same number on your Soul Urge column, you are fortunate indeed. This indicates a common inner desire in life and makes life so much easier for you both.

A QUICK WAY TO ANALYSE SOMEONE FROM THEIR FIRST NAME

A good party trick is to ask someone to think of a famous person (this name can be whispered to the others in the group). All you need is that person's first name and you can tell, in broad measure, the character and destiny of this person. After the laughs have died down, you can then proceed to amaze the party with your 'magical' powers!

The key is to examine the **first vowel** of the first name. Luckily, there are only five vowels (plus the 'y'). The first vowel tells the story. *Refer to the individual numbers in Chapter 1 for further insights.*

FIRST VOWELS

A (1) Many names have the letter A as first vowel (Mary, Barbara, Alison, Margaret, Jane, Alice, Clara, Paul, Barry, David, Graham, etc). This is a pioneer, an original, someone who prefers to lead rather than follow. They are assertive with a keen mind and can be rather stubborn and opinionated. They are good communicators, having a way with words.

E (5) They like to directly experience as much as possible of life. They love change and variety and will always 'have a go'. They love their freedom and, therefore, marriage can be difficult. They can live happily in the physical and spiritual planes.

I (9) They have a broad, idealistic, humanitarian outlook, but desire power over others to make the world a better place. They are intensely emotional, but can be rather selfish. If they suffer from low self-confidence they may go into hiding and retreat into their shell.

O (6) They have a highly developed sense of service and responsibility to others. They are usually self-effacing and reserved. They love fine things in their home and desire harmony in their world. They are born teachers in the widest sense.

U (3) They are charming, easy going people with a touch of class. They are interesting company and keep the party going. But they can be secretive and remote. They are very creative.

The Great Karmic Lesson

This is one of the most important issues to be revealed from your name. When we are born, our soul seeks to gain experience (often through much trial and error) by subconsciously accepting challenges and obstacles. In every incarnation, we have a main lesson to learn. This lesson is indicated by the numbers that are **missing** from your birth name – your Great Karmic Lesson.

For those with no numbers missing (all numbers from 1 to 9 are present), their Great Karmic Lesson is **0**. This does not mean that you are let off the hook this time around, but you are free to choose (again, subconsciously) your own lessons.

Going back to our example, Sarah Elizabeth Moore, we see that the only number missing from her full name is the number **7**. Thus, Sarah's Great Karmic Lesson is **7**.

You and your partner's name may have numbers missing – discover what they are. Then refer to that number below (and if it is a number from 4 to 9, then refer to that number in Chapters 1 and 2).

The Great Karmic Lesson Rule: add up all missing numbers from your birth name. **Do not reduce the number to the single-digit root unless it is greater than 22.**

Write here your Great Karmic Lesson ....

Write here your partner's Great Karmic Lesson ....

You may be surprised to learn what your lessons are. Perhaps you will be disturbed to discover them. Remember, no one is 'condemned' to endlessly repeat any pattern for life. We are all able to transcend our limitations – and that is the great work we all must do.

Since the numbers 1, 2, 3 are very common in most names, it is extremely rare to find a Great Karmic Lesson of 1, 2, or 3. Most Lessons fall between the number 4 and 16, so we'll examine what each Lesson means.

GREAT KARMIC LESSON 4

You doggedly work towards your goals with little enjoyment in life. Emotions are not important to you. You think you have a handle on everything and you do not appreciate challenges to your order and will react with anger and resentment. You are good at maintaining order in the home and at work and are loyal to a fault. You prefer to be left alone doing your job and you positively dislike having to get involved in other people's personal problems.

In love, you are intense, if somewhat stolid. You work hard at being a good provider for your family. If lacking in partner support, you can be led astray by another, to seek a bolstered sense of self-worth.

Lesson: Lighten up, enjoy life more – and stop worrying.

GREAT KARMIC LESSON 5

You are very independent and active, not liking to stay with anything too long and often acting on impulse. You will travel a great deal and have many homes. You will have many unusual experiences, sometimes seeking thrills and spills. You are tempted to over indulge in alcohol, food, chocolate, sex, or drugs, so you need discretion in all things. You have a natural curiosity and inventiveness, but prefer not to work too hard and prefer to make 'easy' money. You are attracted to a sales career.

In love, you have a carefree nature that others are drawn to. You flirt a lot and prefer not to be tied down. You enjoy the thrill of a new relationship. You are aware of your sexual magnetism and use it freely, often confusing your sexual with your emotional needs. You sometimes have a hardness that can hurt your partner and you are not likely to enjoy the confines of a conventional marriage.

Lesson: Find the freedom you seek within.

GREAT KARMIC LESSON 6

You would love to be General Manager of the Universe, but must content yourself with overseeing your family and workplace. Your concern for the world and its tragedies makes you overlook the needs of those closest to you and especially your own. Your generosity to humanitarian causes knows no bounds. Your approach to business is decidedly uncompetitive – you would rather make friends than take advantage of another.

You are often imposed upon by others, but find it hard to distrust anyone. You prefer one lifelong relationship to a string of affairs, but you require the same deep commitment from your partner. You may travel, but you make a comfortable, cosy home everywhere you stay. If your partner loses interest, you will hang in there and suffer a poor marriage rather than confront the nastiness of a divorce.

Lesson: Open your eyes and give to yourself and your loved ones unconditionally.

GREAT KARMIC LESSON 7

This is a common lesson. Around you, there hangs an aura of secrecy, of philosophical questioning, which intrigues others. You must get to the bottom of things quickly and, when you have made up your mind, it is often set in stone. You have an outward appearance of being 'as cool as a cucumber' but, inside, your emotions may be a raging torrent. You guard these feelings jealously, fearing their power. You are very intuitive, but learn to trust it only later in life.

You enjoy business, but are not motivated by money alone. Your analytical mind helps you achieve steady progress, but when your emotions are involved, all of your logical preparations fall apart and you become impulsive, often making rash decisions. You find friendship and relationships difficult ('I want to be alone...') when out of touch with your feelings – but you are very loyal to your few close friends.

You need a partner you can intellectually respect and become fervent once attached. You lose interest if you suspect your partner falling short of your high mental standards and in fact, you may have more of an intellectual companionship than a love affair. You thrive on debate. You dislike the problems and noise created by children.

Lesson: Get in touch with your feelings and thereby deepen your relationships.

GREAT KARMIC LESSON 8

You believe you are destined for greatness and are forever seeking ways to improve your chance of success and boost your ego, but are often unwilling to put in the necessary effort. You can be ruthless and direct, but this hides a basic insecurity and a fear of failure. This can result in bullying of family and colleagues.

You will get to the top of any organisation, but will have difficulties with bosses and managers on the way up. You have creative ideas for the more efficient operation of your business. Unfortunately, at the same time, your own finances may be in a mess.

You need your partner and friends, but act as if they are not that important to you. You are ready to offer advice but, when others come too close to your emotional core, you put up the shutters and quickly change the subject. Your competitive streak does not allow you to accept others for who they are, but for what they have got. This attitude extends to your love relationships as well. Here, your emotional detachment generates indifference – and your relationships suffer. You would do best with a strong, ambitious partner who is able to give you constant boosting.

Lesson: Be more sensitive to the needs of others, and be less materialistic.

GREAT KARMIC LESSON 9

This is one of the most difficult lessons, because it involves recognising and letting go of relationships, of possessive attitudes and of insecurities that do not further your spiritual growth. You seek a

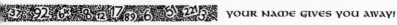

stable marriage and home life, yet there is something deep within that tells you not to become attached to them. You often feel lonely, as if spiritually aware of your isolation. You have high ideals and become despondent when they are not matched in the outside world.

You thrive best in a supportive, inspirational role in business, such as motivation or public relations. You enjoy working on other people's growth. Your circle of friends include people of opposing views and interests. You attract people who trample over your feelings. No matter, your sights are set on bringing a new order to the world. You are idealistic about romance. You will have several platonic relationships and may not ever find the 'ideal' person you so fervently desire.

Lesson: Let go of your personal desires and surrender to the greater will.

GREAT KARMIC LESSON 10

Your considerable energy often produces great success, but you have a constant sense of impending disaster and you often hesitate before making important decisions, fearing the worst. After showing initial enthusiasm for anything new in your life, you can suddenly lose your confidence and become paralysed with fear of failure. You encounter firm resistance when trying to force your opinions on others.

In business, you can swing from having success within your grasp to being on the verge of failure. Your mood swings are also extreme, until you learn to recognise your immense talents are to be used productively and steadily, rather than impulsively. You work best by working solo but as part of a team. You desire leadership, but it is elusive, and you prefer to initiate a new project than to take over something that is already established.

In love, you are changeable and seek a partner who sees your needs and boosts your confidence. You often look for a new affair when feeling insecure. You are best with a partner who is flexible and supportive, since you are not easily domesticated.

Lesson: Think of others more and believe you can make a difference.

GREAT KARMIC LESSON 11

You are very idealistic and intuitive and have a deep feeling for the needs of the world. You have a leaning towards the esoteric side of life (mysticism, the occult or religion) which, later in life, you will study deeply. Paradoxically, you respond well to new ideas, yet you have a deeply conservative streak, which you defend stubbornly. Either clinging to old and tried ways or hugely enthusiastic to a new idea, you expect everyone else to fit in with identical fervour.

You achieve best results using diplomacy and patience. You are not suited to the cut and thrust of business; you are better employed dealing with sorting out other people's problems. You attract friends from diverse backgrounds and can be lead astray by 'spiritual leaders' with dubious motives. In love, you are idealistic and seek a partner who matches your zeal and your own perceived 'perfection'. You are moody at times and can be emotionally volatile, especially when your partner displays less than 'perfect' behaviour.

Lesson: Get off your pedestal and respect the differences between yourself and others.

GREAT KARMIC LESSON 12

Your life is full of sacrifices. You are constantly nagged by feelings of loss – that things around you will suddenly disappear. You therefore suffer as a result of this anguish, and this suffering leads you in later life towards a path of self-discovery. You express this anguish dramatically. Your sacrifices may be in the form of taking care of a relative, or having to step in at work at just the 'wrong' time.

You have a natural artistic and creative flair which you can use for writing and speaking to groups, especially about what you have learned from life. At work, you are often asked to do extra tasks for which others get the laurels. Your restlessness does not allow you to stay in one position for too long and the success and recognition you deserve only come, after much struggle and sacrifice, later in life.

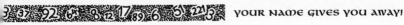

You want to be popular and you love parties. You are spontaneous and excitable and have a great desire to please. In love, you attract rather 'needy' partners and get entangled in complicated relationships with partner, in-laws; in fact, with everybody. You often feel unappreciated and can become easily discouraged.

Lesson: Treat yourself more often and learn to say 'No'.

GREAT KARMIC LESSON 13

You are one of the workers of the world. Not selfishly for yourself, but for the good of everyone. Inwardly, you know this, but you often give up or avoid the work you know you must do. You are here to learn to enjoy work for its own sake and to respect discipline and application. You hold yourself back, as if lacking drive, and exhibit extreme humility that prevents you from 'going for it'. You stay out of the limelight as much as possible.

Early in life, you are not satisfied just working for a living and you may have many setbacks before finding a satisfying career, despite pushing yourself harder than most of your co-workers. You seem to work with your head down and with blinkers on and can be very stubborn in your views. You can be counted upon as a reliable friend and colleague. Your word is your bond.

Your friendships give you much grief. You have several experiences of loyal friends leaving your life suddenly, which brings you great sadness. In love, you have similar experiences. You become frustrated, but you need to see that your fixed attitudes and reluctance to open up emotionally to your partner result in a kind of suspension of the relationship.

Lesson: Learn to be more flexible and accept change – and enjoy your work.

GREAT KARMIC LESSON 14

You are at a major turning point. You will go through much self-examination, many painful experiences, as you move from a life of self-indulgence to one of spiritual awareness. You have sought pleasure at every turn but now, gradually accepting past mistakes, you realise your need for security and roots. You swing between needing complete freedom and needing to have some stability.

Your interests are wide, you have great chances for success in business and work best with others. You are ambitious, adaptable and will change your career several times, often just before reaching great success. Unless you are sensible, you are capable of making and then losing a great deal of money.

Sometimes your self-confidence and exuberance is taken the wrong way and you can ride roughshod over others' feelings without intending to. You move from one romance to another as you confuse sex with love. Until you learn what love means, you should not make lasting commitments.

Lesson: Don't dwell on past mistakes, and accept the spiritual changes you are experiencing.

GREAT KARMIC LESSON 15

This is another difficult lesson. You seem to have mistreated people in a past life, because you often appear humble and contrite. You work hard to present an image of concern for others, yet you are more concerned about yourself. You encounter and battle with many people with massive egos, especially early in life, and can spend years overcoming your sense of guilt. You are emotionally unsettled and can be upset by minor irritations.

You are best working with others in a supportive role. Friends come to you for help and advice. You seek a harmonious and happy relationship, but often get the opposite by attracting a possessive and aggressive partner. Your relationships can suffer because of obstacles created by parental disapproval or not having enough money.

Lesson: Help others out of love, but don't try too hard.

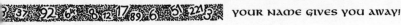

GREAT KARMIC LESSON 16

Yet again, another difficult lesson, since you are constantly looking over your shoulder expecting a catastrophe (refer to the Karmic Number Sixteen in Chapter 1). You live on an emotional knife edge and often make impulsive decisions. You prefer to live on your intellect and can be hasty in making judgments, which you stoutly defend to the last. You have many disappointments early in life.

You are conscientious at work, wanting to be valued for your contribution, rather than being motivated by money alone, despite your materialistic bent. You maintain a somewhat cool detachment with friends and would rather spend time alone. You always seem to be thinking deeply.

In love, you need someone you can respect intellectually, preferably someone with similar views. You search for the perfect relationship and are highly idealistic. You normally find a satisfying relationship later in life when you have learned to balance head and heart.

Lesson: Open your mind and your heart and learn to see how you create your world.

the tides in the affairs of man (and woman)

Your personal nine-year cycle

Not only are names and birthdates numbered, but so are the years that we pass through. Human life is full of **cycles** – the rotation of a sequence of energies, such as the soul cycle of conception, birth, growth, maturity, death, transformation and then back to conception, etc. One of the main cycles of our lives is the nine-year cycle. This is called the **Personal Year** cycle.

Just think how powerful this knowledge is – you can now direct your affairs in line with the requirements of your Personal Year. You can spot 'trouble' coming and get the best out of your experiences during the year. Note that there is a transition period between October and December as the old influences give way to the new. On 1 January, the full force of your new Personal Year will be felt. **This is one of the most important influences in your life**.

The Personal Year rule

Add the numbers of your birth day, your birth month, and the current year. Reduce to a Root Number. This is your Personal Year.

Let's go back to Sarah as an example. If she was born on 17 September, 1970, what is her Personal Year in 1998?

Write day, month and current year: 17   9   1998

Add the digits: $1 + 7 + 9 + 1 + 9 + 9 + 8 = 44 = 8$

Sarah is therefore in an **8 Personal Year** in 1998.

Now, to discover your Personal Year this year, write your birth day, your birth month, and the **current** year. Add up all the digits, and find the root number. This is your Personal Year. Now do the same for your partner. Work out yours and your partner's Personal Years from 1990–2001.

Write both your Personal Years below:

	Personal Year	
	Yours	**Partner's**
1992	......	......
1993	......	......
1994	......	......
1995	......	......
1996	......	......
1997	......	......
1998	......	......
1999	......	......
2000	......	......
2001	......	......

Many of the difficulties you may have with your partner can be understood by differences in your Personal Years. Work with your energies and not against them. Understand your partner's energies this year and see where in the past, you both failed to 'swim with the tide'.

To get an overview of what the requirements of a particular Personal Year are, refer to discussion of that number in Chapters 1 and 2.

Let's look at the Nine-Year Personal Year cycle energies.

PERSONAL YEAR 1

You will feel as if you have the world at your feet, for this is the year to start doing what you have always dreamed of, but never did. If you have always wanted to write a book, go around the world, change your career, change your residence, start a new business, or even get married, there is no better time than now. This is the year to begin practically anything.

It is very much a year for action, not dreaming. You must initiate on your own and lead by doing. You hold the reins of your partnership now, so take courage. Tremendous creative energy is flowing through you which you can hardly contain. It feels as if you have been hibernating and have suddenly sprung to life.

It is no exaggeration that whatever you initiate (or do not initiate) this year will greatly influence your life for the next eight years of your cycle, so plan and act wisely. This is a pivotal year for you.

Key: Just do it!

PERSONAL YEAR 2

This is a year to consolidate your efforts from the previous year. You will feel like taking a well-earned rest from your exertions. It is a time when you will need understanding and tact, and your relationships will become much more important to you. Emotions will be high and progress can be made only by sharing and cooperating. You may feel frustrated that the plans of last year haven't fully matured. Have patience, it is the time to sit back and watch things grow.

It is a year of giving and sharing and seeking harmony. You will find new friends and new relationships. If you have a partner, it is a great time for strengthening your relationship. If single, you may find a new love.

Key: Keep smiling!

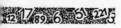

PERSONAL YEAR 3

This is your year – so enjoy it. It is a year to enjoy mixing with people – renewing old friendships and making new ones. You will feel like expressing yourself through the arts. This is a great year for romance and, if single, you will be socially active. But, if single it is best not to tie yourself down with one partner yet.

You will find life rather pleasant this year, but do not allow yourself to drift – you must make a real effort to make positive progress. Allow partner and friends to help you in your work. You will be optimistic and cheerful, so spread good cheer wherever you go. You will have opportunities for travel, making money and enjoying your relationships.

Key: Enjoy life.

PERSONAL YEAR 4

This is a year for getting down to work and attending to practical details. You will not find much time for enjoying life, so be prepared to make some sacrifices and do not initiate any large-scale changes – they have a habit of not working out this year. If changes come along from others, that is fine, since they are likely to be secure. In relationships, a marriage will likely be a happy one provided you do not take the initiative. But typically, the early months of a Personal Year Four relationship will be shaky as many adjustments will need to be made in order to make a firm foundation.

Key: Keep your nose to the grindstone.

PERSONAL YEAR 5

This is a year for adventure and excitement – it's your freedom year after the grind of last year. It is a year of change. You will feel the need to seek out the new and unusual. Go on that round the world tour or change careers. Many partnerships begin to break up in this year if they are not secure. You will feel restless all year but be aware that, by making a major change in one area, you will prompt many changes down the line. By keeping alert and open minded, this year will allow you to clear things up and make a new start.

You will feel impatience when things seem to go slowly or your partner seems to hold you back. The key is to make changes that benefit others as well. You may be confused by all this activity, but go along for the ride – and have fun doing it.

Key: Get out there and explore.

PERSONAL YEAR 6

After the fun and excitement of the Five year, this is a year of responsibilities and duty. Family matters will take precedence and you will need to make adjustments. This is the best year for moving home, getting married or making a serious commitment to your partner. Normally, the Six year is either an up or a down year with your partner and family – there is usually no in-between. Many shaky partnerships break up in this year. It is crucial to approach this year with the right attitude.

You will feel as if the whole world needs you this year. It is not the time for selfishness. If you do not work towards greater harmony, then your world may collapse.

Key: Be accepting.

PERSONAL YEAR 7

In stark contrast to the Six year, the Seven year is your 'desert island' year. You will feel the need to spend much time on your own with your own thoughts. You will go within and will be attracted to meditation, prayer or self-help books. This is not the year for making big changes in your home, your relationships or your business. A good year for going away, spending time in reflection and in seeking spiritual answers. It is not a dull year, for you should expect the unexpected.

By following your inner urges, a goal and plan of great importance will appear, which will normally only be fully realised in the next Personal Year One. You will have difficulties with your partner unless you honestly express your needs and feelings clearly. Others may misunderstand you in your need for solitude. Be careful you do not become a hermit. This is a transition year for you, so do not force issues.

Key: Have understanding and trust your intuition.

PERSONAL YEAR 8

'As ye sow, so shall ye reap' is the key to this year, for you will harvest all the work you have done in the previous years. It is the year of your power and wealth, so this year, you can expand your business, begin a new one, or sell your present one. It is a very materialistic year, but you will need to make great personal effort to 'cash in'. It will not be easy and you need good judgment and a definite plan. Finances may be strained until you reach success, so you need to be realistic about your ability and value.

Spiritually, this is a 'pay off' year where Karmic bills become payable and losses can occur. Do not be too dominant with your partner – try to work together.

Key: Climb that ladder of success.

PERSONAL YEAR 9

This is a year of endings, of sweeping away the rubbish of your life. It is not a year to begin anything new, such as marriage. Any new romance, new business, new friendship started this year will likely not last the year. This is a time for tying up loose ends, for clearing the attic, and for stocktaking. You should be looking ahead to next year, dreaming and making plans ready to launch in your Personal Year One. It is often a time of sorrows with some pain and sacrifice as your affairs come to a head.

Be willing to let go of the old and the undesirable. Have compassion and understanding of others. This could be one of the most wonderful years for you if you accept with love the release of those people and conditions from your life that do not serve you or the greater good.

Key: Take stock and let go.

The Letters of Transit and your Essence

Yesterday, today and tomorrow – the trinity of our lives. Through the Letters of Transit, we can look back, look up and look forward to see where we have been, where we are now and where we are heading. Then we can put into perspective our past, we can understand our present and we can prepare of the future. This is another powerful source of help for us all, since it pinpoints by the year the influences

Age	1	2	3	4	5	6	7	8	9
Sarah	S(1)	A(1)	R(9)	R	R	R	R	R	R
Elizabeth	E(5)	E	E	E	E	L(3)	L	L	I(9)
Moore	M(4)	M	M	M	O(6)	O	O	O	O
Age	10	11	12	13	14	15	16	17	18
	R	R	A(1)	H(8)	H	H	H	H	H
	I	I	I	I	I	I	I	I	Z(8)
	O	O(6)	O	O	O	O	O	R(9)	R
Age	19	20	21	22	23	24	25	26	27
	H	H	S(1)	A(1)	R(9)	R	R	R	R
	Z	Z	Z	Z	Z	Z	Z	A(1)	B(2)
	R	R	R	R	R	R	R	E(5)	E
Age	28	29	30	31	32	33	34	35	36
	R	R	R	R	A(1)	H(8)	H	H	H
	B	E(5)	E	E	E	E	T(2)	T	H(8)
	E	E	E	M(4)	M	M	M	O(6)	O
Essence	16/7	19/1	19/1	19/1	10/1	17/8	14/5	16/7	22

and opportunities of our lives (the Personal Year gives us the broad direction of our lives, while the Letters of Transit gives us an idea of the opportunities presented).

The method is based upon the transits of each letter of your birth name. Each letter will have an influence for the number of years equal to the number associated with the letter. For instance, if you are under the influence of the letter E, that will last for five years. We begin with the first letter of each name at the age of one and construct a chart as follows (again taking the name Sarah Elizabeth Moore as an example):

Sarah is age 28 in 1998. Her Letters of Transit in 1998 are R, B and E. These add up to 16. This number is called her **Essence**. Note that Sixteen reduces to the Root Number Seven. Sixteen is a Karmic Number and is rather unfortunate, since it means Sarah can expect some sudden shocks this year. For her, 1999 will be much better, since the Letters of Transit add up to 19, when she will find great freedom and happiness. Note that when Sarah is age 36, she will be in an Essence of Master Number 22 - a particularly significant year in her life.

In this way, you can examine your own and your partner's life as far backwards and as far forwards as you care to.

The Essence table

1 Surging energy to begin new projects, to travel, to change career.
2 Consolidation with family and friends important, and patience necessary.
3 Get involved with the arts. Good time socially and romantically. Good marriage vibrations.
4 Nose to the grindstone year. Do not initiate any major changes.
5 Unexpected new directions open up, particularly with friends and partners.
6 Family duty year. Great marriage vibrations; also changes in home.
7 Not favourable for major changes with partner, home or business. Go within.

8 Active year for building your finances and position.
9 A finishing year with losses indicated. No major starts romantically. Good for travel.
11 Creative year best spent on spiritual and awareness studies. Not good socially.
22 A pivotal year. Great success especially with large-scale humanitarian projects.

Let's go ahead and work with your name and your partner's. Construct a similar chart with nine columns headed 1–9, 10–18, 19–27, 28–36, etc. as we have done above. Write the letters of your names (if you have three names, you will end up with three rows of letters) for the number of years that the number of the letter indicates. When you have finished a name, start again. Examine the current year. What is your Essence? What is the Essence of your partner? If they are similar, you will be paddling in the same direction. Sometimes, they will be dissimilar (such as an Essence of 3 alongside an Essence of 7). Armed with this knowledge, you both will be better prepared to face the challenges of every year. Work out yours and your partner's Essence for the years 1995–2002.

	Yours	Partner's		Yours	Partner's
1995	......	......	1999	......	......
1996	......	......	2000	......	......
1997	......	......	2001	......	......
1998	......	......	2002	......	......

5

YOUR COMPATIBILITIES WITH OTHERS

The Relationship Number

By far the most important link between you and your partner – that connection which gives the most intense energies and issues – is that concerning your **Life Purpose** with theirs. We have many other points of connection as revealed by the numbers within our individual 'charts', but it is through your Life Purpose that the highest connections are made. As simple as it seems, your main relationship energies are revealed as the sum of both of your Life Purpose numbers. This number is called your **Relationship Number**. Let's do a quick example.

Say you are working **3** as your Life Purpose and someone comes into your life who is working **5** as their Life Purpose (you need to ask their birthdate). Here, the energies of the relationship is the sum of your **3** and their **5**, so your **Relationship Number** is **8**. What do we know of this number? Referring to a description of this number in Chapter 1 and 2, we can say that your main issues will be about **abundance** (do we have enough possessions, or do we want more?) and **power** (do we battle over who is in charge, or do we share our power wisely?). Note that all relationships that have the Relationship Number **8** will have these issues as central (e.g. a Life Purpose **1** with a **7**, a **2** with a **6** and so on).

Here are a few examples:

Your Life Purpose	Partner's Life Purpose	Relationship Number
2	5	7
7	9	16/7
		(double-digit numbers
		reduce to root)
1	6	7
1	9	10
2	9	11
		(11 is Master Number)
5	5	10
8	6	14/5
6	7	13/4

Note the interesting combination:

9	9	18/9

The Relationship Rule

**Relationship Number = your Life Purpose Number
plus your partner's Life Purpose Number**

The Relationship Number describes the important issues and energies between you and you partner.

Try a few examples:

If you have a serious love relationship, we can work out your Relationship Number:

Your Life Purpose Number ...... + Your partner's Life Purpose Number ......

= Your Relationship Number ......

Your Relationship Number should be one of the numbers between **2** and **12**.

Let's now examine the various issues for each of the eleven Relationship Numbers. Remember, whatever relationship we are in, we can choose to work in the positive or the negative (or more

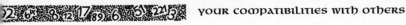

commonly, a mixture of both). As we mature, we consciously choose to move out of the negative into the positive. Our relationships are really an intensive course in individual maturity and growth, often providing us with our most inescapable challenges.

It is useful first to work out the Relationship Number with your partner and then review the description for that number in Chapter 1 and earlier in this Chapter. This will give you some background information for the type of relationship you have. Then go to the description of the Relationship Number outlined below. This will give you and your partner a means of identifying those issues that may be preventing you from growing and developing, if that is indicated. If you feel stuck in a relationship, it will help to work it more in the positive. For each Relationship Number, several suggestions for growth are made. It is very powerful to know which issues specifically require attention.

Notes:

1 The Number One does not appear as a Relationship Number, but the Number Ten does.
2 The Number Eleven stays as a Master Number.
3 Reduce Relationship Numbers from Thirteen to Eighteen to the respective Root Number (from Four to Nine). As an example, say the Relationship Number is $8 + 7 = 15$. Reduce the Fifteen to the root ($1 + 5 = 6$). The Relationship Number is **6**.

The Relationship Number 2

Working in the Positive

There is mutual, loving support and a great sense of loyalty and cooperation present. Decisions are made by diplomacy and tact, as opposed to one partner 'laying down the law'. Each partner complements (and compliments) the other, making a very powerful harmonious union. Each partner respects the opinions and preferences of the other. Each partner feels secure within him or herself, and within the relationship. They spend a great deal of time together, happily enjoying each other's company.

WORKING IN THE NEGATIVE

There is much emotional upset with frequent outbursts and heated arguments. There is confusion about the direction and purpose of the relationship. Responsibilities are blurred, with the 'right-hand' not knowing what the 'left hand' is doing. There is a battle between one partner's mind and the other's emotions.

SUGGESTIONS FOR GROWTH WITHIN THE RELATIONSHIP

- Ask each other what it is you enjoy doing together – and agree to do more of these things.
- Discover your needs and your partner's – introduce more 'give and take' to balance your needs with your partner's.
- Agree to share responsibilities more formally (write a list?) – but stay flexible.

THE RELATIONSHIP NUMBER 3

WORKING IN THE POSITIVE

There is a deep bond where feelings are clearly and openly expressed without fear of criticism. Conversations are joyfully stimulating with complete honesty of expression. The relationship attracts friends from diverse walks of life, with much travel. Many Three relationships produce children, who are blessed to be born to parents who nurture them with sensitivity to their needs. There is a love of life and enthusiasm within the relationship. Partners living together create a warm, beautiful home and entertain frequently.

WORKING IN THE NEGATIVE

Each partner is 'needy' with not enough 'give and take'. One or both partners is overly sensitive to perceived hurts from the other. There is a feeling of self-pity and lack of self-confidence with one or both partners. Feelings are withheld and suppressed with depression common. Partners say what they think instead of what they feel.

SUGGESTIONS FOR GROWTH WITHIN THE RELATIONSHIP

- Ask each other whether you each truly listen (with the heart, not the head) to each other, or whether you talk past each other.
- Do you mutually support each other to express yourselves openly, or are there hidden sensitivities which can overcome self-doubt?
- Ask yourselves whether you honestly share your feelings.

THE RELATIONSHIP NUMBER 4

WORKING IN THE POSITIVE

There is a strong foundation within the relationship, with you and your partner each feeling secure. Each partner contributes towards mutual goals with an honest exchange of views. From the secure foundation, the relationship contributes in a practical way to projects that benefit others.

WORKING IN THE NEGATIVE

There are frequent disputes over children and relatives. There is no sense of purpose or direction, with conflicting ideals. One partner feels a heavy burden of responsibility and obligation that is not matched by the other partner. There is a a feeling of stubbornness within the relationship, which seems 'stuck'.

SUGGESTIONS FOR GROWTH WITHIN THE RELATIONSHIP

- What are some practical steps we can take to move to where we both would like to be?
- Do we make decisions purely logically, or do we take into account how we both truly feel?

The Relationship Number 5

Working in the positive

There is a feeling of excitement when together, even doing day-to-day chores. New experiences are welcomed with variety being 'the spice of life'. Both partners feel free to be themselves despite a sense of interdependence.

Working in the negative

Partners feel a 'tug of war' – a feeling of can't live with and can't live without each other. There is either a trapped feeling, or a sense of going in too many directions at once. Partners are frequently on an emotional roller coaster with each other.

Suggestions for growth within the relationship

- Do we need to reorder our activities and, if so, can we find the discipline to carry it out?
- When we want to do something different, what is stopping us?

The Relationship Number 6

Working in the positive

There is a feeling of optimism and confidence as both partners work towards a shared vision of the future. Both partners work together in unselfish service and support of their family and others.

Working in the negative

The partners believe the other is failing to live up to their expectations and experience a sense of failure. One partner attempts to 'change' the other, especially in appearance and habits. Their conversations are full of petty carpings and criticisms.

Suggestions for growth within the relationship

- What do we like about each other, and can we build on that?
- What is it we want to accomplish together?
- Can we accept each other the way we are?

The Relationship Number 7

Working in the positive

There is a deep feeling of trust based upon an unspoken understanding. Both partners are open with each other, especially emotionally. Both partners allow each other great freedom to work alone and to process events internally.

Working in the negative

There is much misunderstanding and mistrust of each other with important secrets well hidden. Each partner relies on the other to fulfil itself – a co-dependent relationship. One or both partners live in fear of being betrayed.

Suggestions for growth within the relationship

- Are there hidden secrets we are keeping from the other because of shame?
- Can we develop greater trust in each other?

The Relationship Number 8

Working in the positive

Power is freely shared between partners for the good of the relationship. Both work towards greater abundance for their family. There is a feeling of harmony in the home with always a great plan afoot.

WORKING IN THE NEGATIVE

Many struggles over who is in charge, with little give and take. Scattered direction means frequent financial difficulties.

SUGGESTIONS FOR GROWTH WITHIN THE RELATIONSHIP

- Do we feel the need to dominate our partner? Can we introduce power sharing?
- How can we feel a greater sense of abundance (wealth isn't only measured in terms of money).

THE RELATIONSHIP NUMBER 9

WORKING IN THE POSITIVE

There is a great feeling of mutual compassion and tolerance. There is total respect for the differences between partners. Both partners are honest with each other and lead by example.

WORKING IN THE NEGATIVE

Partners feel lonely and cut off from each other. Partners have strongly held opposing views on most things and frequently clash. Both feel limited within their relationship.

SUGGESTIONS FOR GROWTH WITHIN THE RELATIONSHIP

- How can we learn to love the differences with our partner?
- Can we appreciate that we do not know what is best for the other?
- Can we eliminate the habit of imposing our opinions on the other?

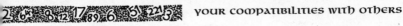

The Relationship Number 10

Working in the Positive

Partners feel a special closeness (as if they were brother and sister in a previous life?). Together, they work creatively with great passion and energy.

Working in the Negative

Both feel suppressed irritation with the other with frequent arguments. The partners are competitive towards each other with hurt feelings common. There is often a battle of wills.

Suggestions for Growth within the Relationship

- Can we learn to express our feelings more freely without fear of intimidation?
- How can we work closer together with more energy?

The Relationship Number 11

Working in the Positive

Both partners generate considerable creative energy and can achieve anything they want. They co-operate effectively without arguments about who does what and when. Together, they work on projects that light other people's lives.

Working in the Negative

Their considerable energies may be blocked and then released by violent means. They have intense love/hate feelings with their partner with a high sexual energy. There is a constant battle of egos and wills.

SUGGESTIONS FOR GROWTH WITHIN THE RELATIONSHIP

- Can we use our considerable energy more creatively and positively?
- Can we turn our arguments and battles around and agree to work towards a common goal?

THE RELATIONSHIP NUMBER 12

WORKING IN THE POSITIVE

There is a feeling of sharing the load through unselfish contribution. Partners complement each other and make up a productive unit. There is honest and open expression of feelings.

WORKING IN THE NEGATIVE

Partners feel separated and fragmented with a feeling of going nowhere. There is considerable frustration with stifled energies. There is little sense of give and take.

SUGGESTIONS FOR GROWTH WITHIN THE RELATIONSHIP

- How can we support each other more positively?
- How can we learn to give more to the relationship?

Do you feel at home in your house?

It surprises many to know that the number of your house (or name, if it has no number) has a distinct bearing on your happiness in living there. Of course, we all wish to be happy in our homes, but we use our homes for a variety of purposes. If you wish to have an active social life, get down to making a fortune, or want to study, what are the best numbers for you?

A great deal of unhappiness in moving home can be avoided by understanding your current needs and seeking a house with the appropriate number. If you are unhappy with your home, but cannot move, try to understand and work with the requirements of your home.

Each house carries the energy of the number of the house on the street. Your house wants to express itself in that way and, if you co-operate with it, you will make substantial progress. Remember that not all numbers are equally beneficial. To obtain the basic energies of a house, simply take the number and reduce to a Root Number. For instance, 34 Lime Avenue is a **7** house. What is the number of your home?

For each House Number, there are certain Relationship Numbers (see Chapter 5) that will be especially favoured by those living in this house. These favoured relationships are indicated for each House Number. Reduce Compound Number addresses to the Root Number.

If you live in a house with a name and no number, simply analyse the name into its letters and add up the numerical value of all the letters in the name. For instance, say you live in Glebe Cottage, this name has the value of **3**, so the House Number is Three.

fAVOUReD RelAtionship NumBers

house NumBer 1

This is a home for self-motivated, independent-minded people. It encourages originality, creativity and determination in all who live under its roof. A strong character is necessary to live here. There always seems to be something going on, with many unusual and interesting happenings. It is a hive of activity.

Favoured Relationship Numbers: Five, Eleven and especially Ten.

house NumBer 2

This is a home for socially active, refined, gracious people, who delight in sharing and entertaining. Simplicity is the key here – in furnishing as well as in lifestyle. Difficulties are overcome by co-operation and diplomacy. The home encourages a spiritual approach to life with concern for others. Many interesting experiences occur through friendships and partnerships in business. Careful attention to detail is required. Hasty actions are counter productive; time must be given to allow proper development. When the house is kept clean and tidy, it is a very charming home.

Favoured Relationship Numbers: Six, Eleven and especially Two.

house number 3

This is a home that needs to radiate happiness and cheer. It can be an imposing home, but has an atmosphere of friendliness and comfort. The home encourages artistic expression. But the temptation is present to indulge in extravagances without putting out the necessary efforts to earn them. There is a temptation to search for love and romance outside of the relationship and, if this happens, there will be much unhappiness throughout the home.

The home loves romance, but requires truth and loyalty. A great house for entertaining and having fun, especially with children.

Favoured Relationship Numbers: Five, Twelve and especially Three.

house number 4

This is a serious home where qualities of courage, steadiness and security are demanded. Residents should be practical minded, using established routines and methods to achieve success. Family problems will require constant attention and can be handled using good common sense. Underlying the wholesomeness there is an atmosphere of fun and good nature. This home encourages civic duties and contribution to the community.

Too much caution can breed stagnation, so you must allow some flexibility and let your hair down sometimes. But this is a home where responsibilities need to be exercised and where respect by the community needs to be earned. It is an excellent number (as is the Eight) for a home or office to 'attract' business success.

Favoured Relationship Numbers: Eight and especially Four.

house number 5

This is a home for active, progressive people that love the new and get a thrill from changing conditions. Routines have a short life here, as there is so much going on, sometimes at a frantic pace. You have many interests and activities, which prevent a smooth running of the household. There is much coming and going and never a dull moment. This home loves enterprise and growth (a great home for plants and children).

Despite all this activity, haste still makes waste and impatience will not be rewarded. It is best if you take time out occasionally to relax and slow down.

Favoured Relationship Numbers: Three, Ten and especially Five.

house number 6

This is a home for family and domestic matters. It encourages strong family ties, love of children and family traditions. When these are lived up to, the home radiates a love, a welcome, and a beacon of service to others. It is not a home for individualised efforts, for progress is made by the whole family working together. The family is bound by a deep sense of belonging and a broad humanitarian perspective.

Too much regard for self or a jealous guarding of one's possessions will result in disharmony and discord. You should contribute to the welfare of your community in practical ways.

Favoured Relationship Numbers: Two, Nine and especially Six.

house number 7

This is a home for those with a need for solitude and for quiet reflection. It is not a home for thrashing out one's problems or having heated arguments. It likes people of an enquiring mind and a studious disposition. It is a home full of pride and dignity. It requires strength of character and self-reliance.

All students of any age are welcomed here, particularly if they seek knowledge for its own sake. It is not a home for you if you do not care to live alone.

Favoured Relationship Numbers: Four and especially Seven.

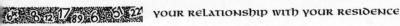

house number 8

This is a home for confident, important people, who are focussed on their goal and who have learned self-control. It is a house of business activity as well as having a domestic side. The home requires good, sound business judgment for its efficient running. Great harmony can be achieved when you undertake business activity for the good of the community as well as your own. Repeated good works bring considerable recognition. This home is very suitable for lawyers and others of authority.

The home is usually more lavishly appointed than most and isn't normally a cosy one. In fact, some Eight houses are more like palaces than comfortable homes. While living here, it is best not to force the pace, otherwise you run the risk of becoming a 'workaholic'. As with the Four, the Eight is an excellent number for home or office for attracting business success.

Favoured Relationship Numbers: Ten, Four and especially Eight.

house number 9

If you are a person that loves people from all classes and nations without prejudice, this is the home for you. This home encourages compassion, tolerance and a fine understanding in all things. For when you have these qualities while living in this home, love and abundance are yours. It is a home to provide inspiration for the highest of ideals and goals. Lovers of beauty, refinement and the arts are welcomed here.

It is a home which demands the highest standards of personal integrity. Living below your potential in this regard will bring unhappiness and sorrow.

Favoured Relationship Numbers: Six, Eleven and especially Nine.

What is your Relationship Number? Are you living at a favourable address? Are you living up to its requirements? If you are planning to start a life with your partner and are searching for a home, keep in mind your favourable House Numbers while house hunting.

Your town or city number

We are all familiar with the idea that certain places carry a certain quality. For instance, many say that 'London is a great place to visit, but I wouldn't want to live there'. This shows that many of us have a love-hate relationship with London. Therefore, there is a sense of **duality** in the place. This duality shows up when we examine the numerology of London.

Let's examine the name 'London' in greater detail. As we do for a person's name, we can find the Soul, the Personality, and the Expression for the city (see Chapter 3). First, we write the letters and put the numbers of the *vowels* above and the numbers of the *consonants* below:

| | 6 | | 6 | | = 12 = 3 = SOUL |

L O N D O N

| 3 | | 5 | 4 | | 5 | = 17 = 8 = PERSONALITY |

29 = 11 = EXPRESSION

So, London has a **3** Soul, an **8** Personality and an **11** Expression. For anyone who has yet to visit London and knows nothing about it, they could see (**3** Soul) that it is a light hearted place where many go to have fun with others – the West End is full of cinemas, theatres, restaurants. It is a serious place where money is made and the law is administered (**8** Personality) – London is the financial hub of Europe and seat of government of the UK. Already, we see a duality. And to cap it all, it has the split personality of an **11** Expression.

Therefore, London is an interesting mix of entertainment (the **3** Soul) and serious business (the **8** Personality). The **11** Expression requires London to be a spiritual centre, shining light into the world, and it is.

Here is another interesting example – Edinburgh.

```
      5   9      3            = 17 = 8 = SOUL
    E D I N B U R G H
      4   5 2    9 7 8        = 35 = 8 = PERSONALITY
                               52 = 7 = EXPRESSION
```

We see that Edinburgh is a very interesting place indeed with the **8** Soul and Personality and the **7** Expression. As we have learned, the energies of the Seven are far removed from those of the Eight.

While the city has a seriousness of demeanour, maintaining an authoritative, business like and impressive interior and exterior (the **8** Soul and Personality) it also has an intensity for scientific investigation (the **7** Expression). Edinburgh is actually an interesting combination of a legal and business centre for Scotland alongside having many world-class schools of learning. Unfortunately, one of the negative aspects of the Seven energy is a tendency to retreat into alcohol and drugs.

Where do you live? Discover the Soul, the Personality and the Expression of your town or city of residence. Are you living up to its requirements? Have you lived in several places? What has been your experiences of living there? See if you can understand their energies in the light of what you have learned.

YOUR COUNTRY OF RESIDENCE NUMBER

In just the same way as with your town or city, the country where you live also asks you to live in accord with its requirements. Here, the influence is less immediate, as the intensity of the influences move from your name, to your home, to your town/city, to your country. Let's take the example of Britain.

We are familiar with the 'British' Empire (note that it wasn't called 'The United Kingdom Empire', or the 'English Empire'). The ancient peoples that lived in Roman Britain were called Britons, so we shall use the name 'Britain' to represent the land where the British live. Let's see what the Soul, the Personality and the Expression are and see if they match up with popular impressions of the land.

$$9 \quad 1 \: 9 \qquad = 19 = \underline{1} = \text{SOUL}$$

B R I T A I N

$$2 \: 9 \quad 2 \qquad 5 \qquad = 18 = \underline{9} = \text{PERSONALITY}$$
$$37 = \underline{10} = \underline{1} = \text{EXPRESSION}$$

We see right away that Britain is a land which has a sunny soul (the **19/1** Soul), is a leader in creative progress in the world, has a unique destiny and has an indomitable spirit. Matched with this is the tolerance, the compassion for others and the humanitarianism (the **9** Personality) of the spiritual leader. The **10/1** Expression compounds the leadership qualities of the **1** Soul.

Take another example: Egypt. This is a very interesting name, since three of the five letters are sevens (the g, y and p). We know that Egypt was home to one of the most advanced civilisations in our history. The ancient culture and religion still hold a fascination and a mystery for us today. Let's analyse the name:

$$5 \quad 7 \qquad = 12 = \underline{3} = \text{SOUL}$$

E G Y P T

$$7 \quad 7 \: 2 \qquad = 16 = \underline{7} = \text{PERSONALITY}$$
$$28 = \underline{10} = \text{EXPRESSION}$$

We see that Egypt has a **3** Soul (easy going, fertile, expressive) with a **7** Personality (spiritual, scientific, mysterious) and a **10** Expression (creative, a leader, innovative).

Note that the Seven personality is emphasised by the presence of the three seven letters.

Do you agree that these qualities very much describe Egypt and its people and civilisation? Which country do you live in? Analyse its name (using its standard English name) and see if the numbers contained accurately describe it.

The numerology of the transition period — the Universal Year Cycle

In Chapter 4, we saw how we all pass through a nine-year cycle with each Personal Year placing requirements on us. For humanity as a whole, we have a **Universal Year** cycle as well. This is given by the calendar year we are living in. For instance, 1997 was an **8** Universal Year (1 + 9 + 9 + 7 = 26 = **8**). So, not only do we have to deal with our own Personal Year vibrations, we all live under the Universal Year energies as well. The vibrations of the Universal Year are apparent on national and international scales.

While our Personal Year energies can be pictured as the internal energies we are working with, the Universal Year energies can be seen as energies streaming on to Earth from the cosmos.

Because 1997 was an **8** Universal Year, the global energy was one of judgments, especially Karmic ones. It was a year of harvest, where we reaped what we had sowed in the previous years. Can you look back at the major events in your country and the world and understand them from the perspective of the Eight energies (refer to Chapter 1)?

Here are the Universal Years for the transition period going into the Third Millennium:

Universal Years	
1996 – **25/7**	2000 – **2**
1997 – **26/8**	2001 – **3**
1998 – **27/9**	2002 – **4**
1999 – **28/1**	2003 – **5**, etc.

A significant feature of the Third Millennium is that **beginning in the year 2000, we have a 'pure' energy at work**. Notice that during the late 1900s, the Universal Year is a Compound Number (in the 1990s, the Universal Year from 1990 to 1999 is 19, 20, 21, 22, 23, 24, 25, 26, 27, 28 – all Compound Numbers). Starting in the year 2000, the Universal Year is a pure Root Number energy (2000 = 2 + 0 + 0 + 0 = **2**, a Root Number). This will have important consequences for children born early in the next millennium.

We see that 1998 is a **9** Universal Year – a year of ending, of losses and of clearing out. It is not a good time for major new undertakings. The following year, 1999, is a **1** Universal Year – a year of new starts, new energy and new directions. The year 2000 is a **2** Universal Year – a year of consolidation. In purely numerological terms, the new energy of the Third Millennium starts to be felt in late 1998.

Also, we are moving out of the Second Millennium into the Third Millennium. For the past thousand years, we have been under the Two energy (see Chapter 1) – a time of tensions and drama. Conflicts between nations have been largely resolved using war – a result of a mode of thinking which emphasises the differences between people, thereby breeding fear and insecurity. As we move into the more healing and holistic Three energy, this destructive mode of thought will gradually disappear and conflicts will be resolved more and more by co-operative give and take.

As we move out of the twentieth century into the twenty-first century, this is also a move out of a **2** energy into a **3** energy. Also, strictly speaking, the twentieth century ends on 31 December, 1998 (which is a **9** Universal Year – a year of endings!). The reason it does not end on 31 December, 1999 is that we begin counting centuries after Christ from 1 January, Year 0, so that the first century AD ends on 31 December 98 (this is an exact span of 100 years). Thus, the strictly accurate time of transition into the twenty-first century (and into the Third Millennium) coincides with the beginning of a **1** Universal Year on 1 January, 1999.

Implications for our relationships

As we have been under the overall influence of the Two energy for many generations, we have had our share of difficulties with our relationships. Recall from Chapter 1 that the Two is ruled by the moon and is the archetype of the feminine principle. People under the Two vibration are prone to illusion and self-deception. As we have seen, the twentieth century (**2** energy) has often been a time of division, of race hatred and of religious wars. Our collective way of thinking has created the illusion that we are all distinct and separate. This illusion has bred fear and this fear has made our relationships difficult.

In this climate of fear and separation, relationships have often been the battle ground for the realisation of these fears. Towards the end of twentieth century, we have seen the divorce rate at very high levels and single parenthood taken for granted.

What can we expect as we move into the Third Millennium? The more balanced energy of the **3** vibration will mean a moving away from the feelings of separation towards a feeling of oneness. We will approach our relationships not so much from the question of 'What can my partner do for me?', but from 'What can we both contribute so as to produce a whole?' There will be a move towards creative co-operation and away from destructive competition.

Parents of children to be born early in the Third Millennium have seen the destruction of family stability in the late twentieth century and will not want that for their children. They will be motivated to respond to the positive aspects of the 3 energy, rather than the negative. Remember that 3 is a very good marriage and partnership vibration.

Because humanity is passing through so many transitions at the same time – into the Third Millennium, into the twenty-first century, into the Age of Aquarius – we can expect a continuation of disruptive energies. The old certainties are being thrown out and we haven't yet seen much of the new ones. But this is giving each of us an opportunity to examine our lives, and to get in touch with what it is we are here to do – our Life Purpose and our Soul Urge.

Children born early in the Third Millennium are blessed

As we saw earlier, the year 2000 has the pure **2** energy. Those children born on 1 January, 2000 have a pure **4** energy as Life Purpose (with a **1** Life Path). The pure Root Number Life Purpose energy has not appeared for hundreds of years. This is very significant. Let's do a few examples:

Birthdate	Life Purpose	Birthdate	Life Purpose
1 Jan, 2000	**4**	1 Jan, 2001	**5**
8 Jan, 2000	**11** (Master Number)	1 Jan, 2002	**6**
1 Feb, 2000	**5**	1 Jan, 2003	**7**
1 Mar, 2000	**6**	1 Jan, 2004	**8**
1 Apr, 2000	**7**	1 Jan, 2005	**9**
1 May, 2000	**8**	1 Jan, 2006	**10**
1 June, 2000	**9**	1 Jan, 2007	**11**
1 July, 2000	**10** (Master Number)	1 Jan, 2008	**12/3**, etc.

We see that from the year 2000 until 2007, many babies will be born with pure Root Number and pure Master Number energies. Remember from Chapter 2 that all people living today who were born in the nineteenth and the twentieth centuries have a Compound Life Purpose energy. This is because the year of birth always starts with '18--' or '19--'.

What does this mean for children born at this time? People born before 31 December, 1999 **have a compound number Life Purpose energy, such as 27/9.** This means that when young, this person must work with the issues thrown up by the 2 vibration, and as he or she matures, the issues of the 7 then need to be faced. Later in life, if both of these energies have been dealt with, then the issues of the 9 can be tackled.

For those born with a Life Purpose of a pure root number, such as 9 (say having a birthdate of 6 January 2000), this person will have no other major Life Purpose issues to work with, except the 9. The implications are far reaching.

With only one Root Number Life Purpose, the person's growth will not be held back by the need to learn lessons of the two numbers making up a Compound Life Purpose energy. That person will then be able to express himself or herself with the full power of their Life Purpose energy. They will be more aware of their destiny and their connection with all others. Under the healing 3 energy (Third Millennium, twenty-first century), these people will be instrumental in leading humanity away from darkness and into the light. The healing 3 energy will be at its most effective during 2001, when the Universal Year is 3.

Not only will children born early in the Third Millennium be blessed, but so will their parents, who will need to be aware of the special work they are being asked to do.

> *'The Book of Nature is written in Number'.*
> Galileo Galilei

Question: *What is the most recent birthdate of someone with a pure Root Number Life Purpose and Life Path?*

Answer: *1 October, 1600. Life Purpose is 1 + 1 + 0 + 1 + 6 + 0 + 0 = 9. Life Path = 1.*

fURThER READING

A good basic overview of numerology: Aracarti, Kristyna, *Numerology for Beginners*, Hodder & Stoughton, 1993.

One of the classics of numerology and very readable by one of the masters of American numerology: Jordon, Juno, *Numerology – The Romance in your Name*, De Vorss and Co. USA.

Another classic from America by a prolific US numerologist, although it is now twenty years old: Buess, Lynn, *Numerology for the New Age*, Light Technology Press, USA.

Yet another American modern classic by a great teacher: Millman, Dan, *The Life you were Born to Live*, and *Way of the Peaceful Warrior*, H. J. Kramer Inc. Publishers, USA.

A wonderfully quirky numerology book is *Numerology – Key to the Tarot*, Konraad, Sandor, Whitford Press, USA. In this book, Konraad analyses the numerology chart of Sherlock Holmes (and Watson and Moriarty)! Reading this book, you will wonder whether they were fictional or real live historical figures. A splendid testimony to the validity of numerology – even for fictional characters. The book also ties in the strong link between numerology and the Tarot.